⊤ǂxą́ní ǁka !kạ̈ĩ̈, háí ⊢ ǀku ǁ3ka̋ë́m
!khe'au !khwǟi, ha ⊢sé
⊤ẋḁóǹì !khwǟi.

Dreaming the Karoo

Dreaming the Karoo

A people called the /Xam

JULIA BLACKBURN

JONATHAN CAPE
LONDON

1 3 5 7 9 10 8 6 4 2

Jonathan Cape is part of the Penguin Random House group of companies
whose addresses can be found at global.penguinrandomhouse.com

Penguin
Random House
UK

Copyright © Julia Blackburn 2022

Julia Blackburn has asserted her right to be identified as the author of this
Work in accordance with the Copyright, Designs and Patents Act 1988

First published by Jonathan Cape in 2022

penguin.co.uk/vintage

A CIP catalogue record for this book is available from the British Library

ISBN 9781787332171 (hardback)
ISBN 9781787332188 (trade paperback)

Typeset in 12.5/16.5 pt Dante MT Std by Jouve (UK), Milton Keynes
Printed and bound in Great Britain by Clays Ltd, Elcograf S.p.A.

The authorised representative in the EEA is Penguin Random House Ireland,
Morrison Chambers, 32 Nassau Street, Dublin D02 YH68

Penguin Random House is committed to a sustainable future for our
business, our readers and our planet. This book is made from
Forest Stewardship Council® certified paper.

MIX
Paper from
responsible sources
FSC
www.fsc.org   FSC® C018179

For Dan Frank
Editor and friend
1954–2021

3.

1.22. wái !!kya !!kuára ē !kú.
Two she springbok.

3. ⊢hunu, "Dassie":
24 April /79. ⊢hái ≠kan'ó

1. "mein tätärŏken 2. 6 t ĕ 4. !kĕ 5. "spas" 7. !kena. !kena "bra̤il" 8. !khä̆ "wata" 9. "mein !!ktän "neu habitatein"

"!a habitatein"

The Karoo: from the !Orakobab word !'Aukarob – Hard Field – is a semi-desert natural region of South Africa. No exact definition of what constitutes the Karoo is available, so its extent is also not precisely defined.

/Xam: the people of the Karoo, south of the Orange River
ka: possessor
!au: a place, a country, dust
/Xam-ka !au: 'the dust of the /Xam', meaning the country belonging to the /Xam
/Xam-ka !ei: the language of the /Xam

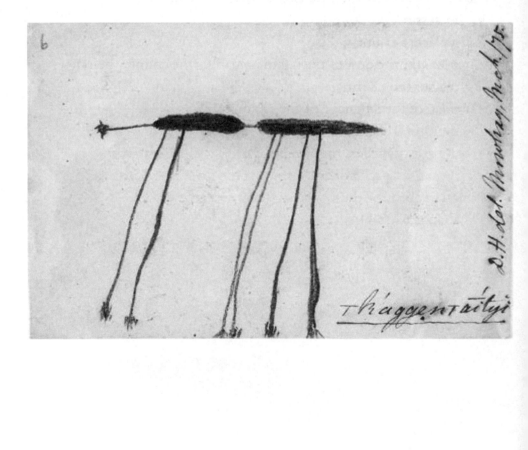

Guide to /Xam pronunciation

X   as in the X of /Xam, is similar to the 'ch' in loch

ʼ   an arrest of breath

:   a lengthened vowel

/   the dental click, made by pressing the tip of the tongue against the teeth and then withdrawing it

//   the lateral click, made with the tongue in the same position

!   the guttural click, made right at the back of the mouth

ǂ   the palatal click, made by pressing the front part of the tongue on the roof of the mouth and then withdrawing it

☉   sounds like a kiss

When I was trying to find a way of stepping into the begin-ning of this book I kept thinking of a shepherd I once knew who lived in a mountainous valley in North Wales. He recited what he said was the oldest Welsh poem and I can still see him standing there in the landscape that belonged to him, speaking in the lan-guage of his people that for me was an incomprehensible and yet powerful sequence of sounds. He then gave a rough translation of what he had said:

> There were once five hundred happy people
> And they were attacked and poisoned
> And after that there was peace and quiet.

I found the poem confusing, which might be why it has remained with me. These people without a name were not apparently doing anyone any harm, so why were they killed, and was it all of them who died: the men, the women, the children and maybe their dogs and chickens as well? Was happiness their crime, or was there some other reason: the presence of gold or silver in the ground beneath their feet perhaps, or the greenness of the grass on which they kept their flocks, or simply the fact of them being there, alive in that place? And do their ghosts remain close by, haunting those who supplanted them?

A Bushman group of hunter-gatherers known as the /Xam – the name spoken with a click on the roof of the mouth followed by a guttural sound as in *loch* – once occupied the whole central interior of South Africa, while other Bushman groups with their own distinct language and territory lived in the north and the west of the country. As a people they have the greatest genetic diversity of any human population and are said to be the ancestors of us all*. Their paintings and engravings can be dated to 10,000 years before this present time, and some are now thought to go back 50,000 years.

The /Xam saw themselves as just one small part of the complexity of the natural world. 'All things were once people', they said, and that belief gave a voice and a dignity to everything that surrounded them, the dead as well as the living, the birds, the animals, the insects and the plants, and also the wind and the rain, the moon and the stars. Everything was speaking to you if you only knew how to listen.

The language of the /Xam, and with that their view of the world and of themselves within the world and the events that were hurtling them to the edge of extinction, would have been lost forever were it not for a German-born philologist called Wilhelm Bleek (1827–75) and his English sister-in-law Lucy Lloyd (1834–1914). Bleek and his extended family were based in Cape Town where he worked as the curator of the Sir George Grey Library, but he also started an independent project to learn the language and the culture of the /Xam from a handful of men who were being held prisoner in the city jail and who later came to stay at his house. His wife's sister Lucy Lloyd worked alongside

---

* In this book I have decided to use the term 'Bushman' and 'Bushmen' throughout. I realise it is a name that carries difficult and sometimes negative connotations, but the alternative use of 'the San' or even 'San Bushmen' is also complicated: experts explain the origin of the word 'San' as derogatory. Everyone I met with in South Africa used the word 'Bushman', and it is how the //Khomani San, the Bushmen of South Africa, refer to themselves.

him, and after his early death she continued with the task for the next thirty-nine years. But whereas Bleek's interest had always been quite academic, she increasingly took on the role of scribe, recording whatever it was that the people wanted to speak about, whether their dreams or their memories, their hopes for the future or their observations of their present circumstances. So even though Wilhelm Bleek's name is prominent within the archive, it is Lucy Lloyd who was responsible for most of the 12,000 notebook pages and it is thanks to her that the voice of the /Xam can be clearly heard.

I

1974 and I had moved into an abandoned warehouse that had once stored crates of tea imported from the pink-stained colonies. The metal-framed windows were blurred with the grime of the city and the wooden floor was covered with a layer of tea-leaf dust. All sorts of objects and bits of furniture had been left scattered about: a table, a coil of rope, an enamelled teapot, a tall cupboard with PAT PAT PAT stencilled on it in white letters and a fat, cloth-bound ledger, which detailed the date on which a pot of tea was brewed from a new consignment and assessed for its quality. The final entry said, 'Tea tasting suspended due to outbreak of War'; the enormity of the event underlined with the steel nib of a dip pen.

I wish I had kept the ledger and the drama of a present and precipitous moment that it was somehow able to contain, but I didn't. It was heavy and cumbersome and eventually I mislaid it, along with much else.

In those days I was working on a book I called *The White Men*. It was a collection of stories that told how Western civilisation appeared in the eyes of the people who were being colonised. Some of the stories were on the edge of being funny – God wore a top hat and lived in a factory called Germany; Paradise was where an unlimited supply of tinned food and rice-in-bags came from – but the underlying theme was always the desecration of the land and the death of a way of life and of the means of staying alive for a whole community of people, whether they were in Africa or the Arctic, Papua New Guinea or New Zealand. As Joseph Conrad put it in *Heart of Darkness*, the colonial process involved plundering new countries of whatever treasures they possessed, 'with no more moral purpose at the back of it than there is in burglars breaking into a safe'.

My research methods were haphazard, even then. I was a member of the London Library and there I could wander through the miles of bookcases, pausing to look at any title that caught my eye. I was in the Anthropology and Ethnography section on the Science and Miscellaneous floor when I came across *Specimens of Bushman Folklore* by Wilhelm Bleek and Lucy Lloyd, published in London in 1911.

I remember lifting the book off the shelf: the solid weight of it, the stiff green cloth binding, the thick pages. Opening it, I was confronted by an incomprehensible language filled with exclamation marks and dashes and hashtags, alongside strange and halting translations of that language into stories and observations, songs and memories. And almost at once I felt myself being pulled into a world and a form of thinking that was nothing like anything I had known before.

> The Bushmen feel a tapping in their bodies when other people are coming . . . a man is altogether still when he feels his body is tapping inside . . . the Bushmen feel people coming by means of it . . . one man feels another man who comes. He says to the children, look around, for grandfather seems to be coming, that is why I feel the place of his body's old wound . . . He feels a tapping at his ribs. He says to the children, the springbok seem to be coming, for I feel the springbok sensation. (//Kabbo)

The book was illustrated with drawings and paintings of birds and animals, plants and people, along with maps and diagrams, including one of a delicate line of dots that represented ostrich feathers mounted on sticks, used to channel a group of springbok towards the hunters who were waiting at the place where the line of feathers curled in upon itself. There were also black-and-white photographs of all the /Xam people whose words were recorded.

I took the book out on loan and because no one else made a request for it I kept renewing it from 4 November 1974 until 9 January 1979. During that time I read it over and over again until some of the texts began to merge with my own memories and experiences. I often gazed at the stern authority on the face of an old man called //Kabbo, the solemn introspection of /A!kunta, the beauty of /Han‡kass'o, the wistful sadness of Dia!kwain, and in time they became as familiar to me as portraits of my own distant and inscrutable ancestors.

And then quite recently I was back in the library and *Specimens of Bushman Folklore* was where it always had been and I borrowed it again, welcoming it home like a stray cat that had been gone for a long time. Now it is here in front of me, stretching its limbs as it were, and the first page still holds the history of our first acquaintance in a long double column of date-of-issue stamps.

//Kabbo

/A!kunta

ǂKasin

!kweiten-ta//ken

/Han‡kass'o

Dia!kwain

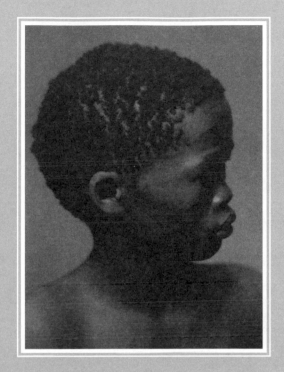

Tamme

Wilhelm Bleek

Lucy Lloyd

II

25 March 2020. I was woken at three in the morning by the ping of a message coming through on my phone. A friend had just died. Before this present time I used to see the word corona as a dizzy circle of light wrapping itself around the full moon or the eclipsing sun.

It's six thirty now. Birdsong. I look outside the window at the gleam of frost on the grass. I get back into bed and listen to the tick of the stove, telling me that if I were to feed the red ash with sticks, it would return to life. My friend was called Kees: an elegant man, Dutch, born in Indonesia, and he spent his early years in a prisoner-of-war camp which gave him an ability to persevere and served him well when he was dying.

I have a tiny headache and a tickle in the back of my throat, but I think it is caused by the concentration of sadness and not by the virus that is racing through every corner of our poor world.

I only returned from the Karoo five days ago. A sudden change of plan and a long drive over unpaved roads and through a hot and desolate land and I got to the airport just in time, making my way onto a crowded plane filled with other people who were exchanging one country for another. The man next to me kept lolling his heavy head upon my shoulder when he slept. He was on the edge of some sort of dementia, not knowing how to fasten his safety belt, which way up to hold a plastic cup, what to do with a spoon, how to find the right words and to speak them. With each new confusion he would turn and give me a loose smile of apology. His wife was in the third seat and she treated him with great kindness, making me think she must have loved him and loved him still.

Now I have come home to the solitude of this house and garden. I was exhausted by the journey and by the shock of what has been happening here during my absence, but I have been writing up my notes and with that I am able to wander in my mind through the places where I have been, the places I had to leave in such a hurry.

Nothing in the Karoo was as I had imagined it might be, except for the strange familiarity of the boulders scattered on low hills across the land: shiny black balls of volcanic magma that had burst out of cracks in the earth's surface in the time of the dinosaurs, or perhaps it was the time of the extinction of the dinosaurs, I can no longer remember. Anyway, the boulders were filled with the energy of their own beginning and looked as if they had just stopped rolling into the position they had chosen for themselves, some isolated and others in clustered groups, some as big as a truck, others no bigger than a cabbage, all seemingly only recently congealed and grown cold.

Long ago, or very long ago – it can be hard to pinpoint the passing of the centuries and the millennia – a group of Bushmen known as the /Xam first started to make elegant images on these stones, cutting, scratching or pecking through the blackness of the surface to reveal a paler colour underneath, in the same way that you might prepare an etching plate. Kudu and ostrich, elephant and praying mantis, the wonderfully humped and dewlapped eland and the shadowy presence of human beings. The drawings are beautiful and vivid, even though the /Xam themselves as they once were and the life they portrayed as it once was have since vanished into what you might call thin air.

The wind blows when we die, for we are the people who have the wind. Clouds come out when we die, and when we die the wind blows dust because it means to blow away our tracks, the tracks with which we walked when there was nothing the matter with us. For if our tracks were visible then it would seem as if we still lived. (Dia!kwain)

III

4 April 2020. I have made a vegetable bed, or at least I think it is made and ready, although pebbles keep appearing on its surface, along with little bundles of tree roots. I have two marrows showing the first of their fan-shaped leaves and waiting patiently to be put in the earth, along with twelve broad bean plants and a pot of wispy French parsley and even wispier dill.

It has been important for me to strengthen the sense of this house being my home, in order to root myself, and the silence of my daily existence, into it. With that in mind, along with the vegetable bed, I have borrowed three nervous guinea pigs from my kind neighbour. When I scoop one of them up and hold it close to my face to breathe in the sweet reassurance of the scent of hay and sunshine, I am reminded of my own childhood and the childhood of my children and of their children too. Tomorrow I hope to build a chicken run, if the chicken wire is delivered, and the same neighbour has promised me two bantam hens and a glowing cockerel. With that my smallholding will be ready to hold my small self steady, as the present moment rolls inexorably into the future, minute by minute, day by night by day again.

I sit in my husband's studio. The door is open and the bright sunshine of this exquisite spring pours in. Six years have passed since he died, but in the quiet of my life here I find he has moved much closer, almost as close as when he first wandered off into whatever other element it is that we go to. He was also good at perseverance in the face of illness, and good at laughter.

A deep breath and I have decided to tell the story of a young /Xam girl and a lioness. I want to use it as a way of entering a very different world and looking around to see what is there. The story somehow makes me feel nostalgic for something I have never known, never could have known; I suppose the presence of a shiny metal button means it must belong in the mid-nineteenth century.

> While Ttai-tchuen was a girl, the mother sent her to fetch a mat and as she came back, there was a lion's house and the lioness had cubs within the house.
>
> As Ttai-tchuen was walking, the lioness sprang out and stood close to her and the girl scooped up a handful of earth, intending to throw dust at the lioness.
>
> The lioness ran back towards the place from which she had come and while she was gone the girl began to cry from fear. Then the lioness again came towards her and

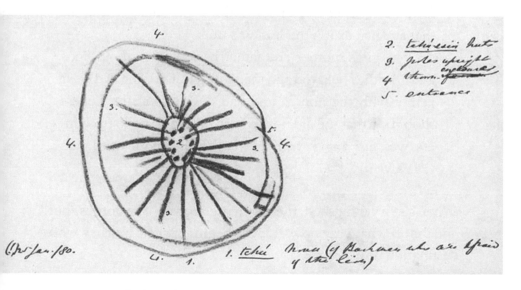

The hut of Bushmen who are afraid of the lion.

sat down in front of her and offered her milk for the girl to drink.

And the girl thought she must not seem as if she was afraid, for a lioness is a creature that desires to see if we mean to attack it and if it sees that we mean to hurt it, then it attacks us, but when it sees that we do not mean to cause pain and we mean to act gently towards it, then it acts gently towards us.

The girl remembered what her mother used to tell her: that a lion is afraid of a thing that reflects light and she thought to herself, 'I will see whether a button will sparkle so that the lion may be afraid of the sparkling.' And she took her button and waved it about and the lioness seemed afraid when the button sparkled under her eyes and she hung her ears as she stood like this and she put her tail between her legs.

After the lioness had left her, the girl went home. And when the dogs ran to meet her, they smelt her scent and she smelt of lion and the dogs were afraid of her.

And her mother said, 'The dogs think she is a real lion, for a lion's scent is on her.' And the girl told her mother that she had drunk the lioness's milk.

The girl's mother and father had told her about lions and how they behaved and therefore she lived. She had dealt gently with the lioness and had desired that the lioness should see that she did not seem to be afraid and so the lioness was not angry with her and dealt gently with her. (Dia!kwain)

When a story is finished, the /Xam used to say, 'The door is shut!', and that is what I say now. It is the beginning of a journey whose destination is uncertain.

IV

9 April 2020. Another day of sunshine. Clouds of white flowers on the blackthorn. The soft hum of bees mixing with the eruption of birdsong and bird comment. The young roots of the twelve broad bean plants, the two marrows and the parsley and dill must be taking hold within the vegetable bed; their leaves shine with something like determination.

The guinea pigs are perhaps a tad more brave, but I am not sure. The delivery of chicken wire has been delayed and so the chickens must wait for their new home. A second friend has died from the virus in this last week, familiar faces floating somewhere close but out of reach. I wake in the early morning of the night and there they are and yet there they are not. The thought of them makes me cry and then I go back to sleep.

> I told my wife I felt my inside aching as the wind blew past, I felt my inside biting. I felt like that when one of my people was dying, my inside always ached when it was one of my people. (Dia!kwain)

Tanya in Cape Town has written to say that the city is in lockdown and every day she takes her dogs on a two-kilometre walk round and round her small garden and John who helps in the house is very pleased with the walking boots I left behind, but yesterday his youngest brother was murdered in the township.

I do not know which township that would be. I passed a number of them from the safe distance of one car or another. The biggest by far was the dense conglomeration of corrugated-iron dwellings erupting like barnacles on a rock beside the main road that leads to the airport. One and a half million people live there, but I could not catch sight of anyone within the closed containment of the area. A few children were playing football on a patch of wasteland beside the motorway, among the flotsam and jetsam of rubbish lying on the grass and clinging to the straggled bushes. A woman was carrying something heavy and two men were sitting in the late sunshine and I was about to catch a plane back home.

On other roads I often saw a man or woman or child walking resolutely in the shadeless heat, close to the noisy zoom of cars and lorries, encapsulated, or so it would seem, in a bubble of solitude. No rush, no turning of the head, just the gentle swing of one step following another.

While I was in Cape Town I stayed for two nights with my friend Tim and his wife Claire. Their six-month-old son is called Adam just like our first ancestor, the one who was taught to make something like a moral distinction between the wild and the tame. Adam valued the land when it produced food crops for him, but saw it as an empty wilderness when it served no practical purpose. He cared for his own domesticated flocks and herds that could be counted and sold and moved wherever he wanted them to go, but he did not care for the countless living creatures that offered him no obedience, and because he had been given dominion over them as well, he must have casually destroyed them whenever it suited him. His children have learned to do the same, from one generation to the next.

Throughout their enormous history, the /Xam never had a sense of dominion over anything: *tchuen ta ku,//kwan ha oa e !k'e* – all things were once people, they said, meaning that everything in the world has equal value.

According to Dia!kwain's grandfather !Xugen-ddi, the quagga was once tame, doing as oxen do, and we stroked and handled it. The man called Chaser of Food, when he saw quagga come grazing out of the water, he went towards the quagga and as he went he called the quagga and the quagga stood . . . and when the quagga thought that he was stroking it nicely, he beat it, laying a stick to it, to give it fear, for when we hunted them . . . he wished that the quagga might spring aside. (Dia!kwain)

The jackal eats people, the jackal's cubs eat people because their parents eat people.

The leopard's cubs do not eat people, because their parents do not eat people.

The silver jackal also do not eat people, because they are silver jackals. They eat mice and hares. (//Kabbo)

All animals marry their own kind and find their place in the world . . . the aardwolf marries a she-aardwolf who lives in a cave . . . He is a man, he is an aardwolf, he speaks, he lives in a cave with aardwolf children, because they always lived in a cave when they were people and talked. (//Kabbo)

Bushmen do not kill frogs, they feel the rain does not fall if we kill frogs. And the place becomes dry. Therefore the Bushmen become lean on account of it, when the rain does not fall and the springbok are not there on account of it . . . and the locusts disappear. (/Han‡kass'o)

V

I've been looking at an old notebook. In December 2017 I was busy with the idea of that thing called progress and how it moves like a sort of demolition machine, getting rid of all traces of the past in order to make way for the future. As an aspect of that thought, I wrote the beginning of a poem based on Lewis Carroll's 'The Walrus and the Carpenter'.

The Banker and the Developer were walking hand in hand,
They laughed like anything to see such quantities of Sand,
'When this is made into Cement,' they said, 'it will be
    grand!'

'With several loans for several years, on interest not one
    penny,
Do you suppose,' the Developer said, 'that we will make our
    Money?'
'I'll bank on it,' the Banker said, they both found that quite
    funny.

In January 2018 I wondered if I might put together a book about the /Xam. 'I could go to the archive in Cape Town, go to the Karoo. I could try to get close to //Kabbo and to the man whose name I forget, who was murdered when he returned to his place . . . There is much sadness in it all, but the enormity of their past will keep me steady and no amount of loss or death can destroy that.'

I then quoted from a /Xam text:

> Finished, our thoughts ascending leave us, while our bodies are those which lie in the earth. (‡Kasin)

And followed that with an account of how the /Xam world began:

> The First at Sitting People were those who first inhabited the earth. Therefore their children are those who worked the Sun. Therefore the people were those who say that the children worked, making the Sun ascend into the sky; while the children felt that their mothers were those who said they should throw the Sun up for them, that the sun might warm the earth for them; that they might feel the Sun's warmth; that they might be able to sit in the Sun.
>
> Before the Sun had been thrown up into the sky, his shining had been only at his own house. The rest of the country was as if the sky was very cloudy; as it is when the Sun is now behind the clouds. The sky then was dark. The shining came from one of the Sun's armholes as he lay down with one arm lifted up. When he put down his arm, darkness fell everywhere. When he lifted it up again, it was as if dawn came. (//Kabbo)

I did nothing more for several months until I was talking with my Dutch friend Sandra about the history of the Boers in South Africa. She helped me to translate some Dutch texts which brought me closer to understanding what was happening to the /Xam as the nineteenth century unfolded. By the 1920s you could say that they no longer existed as a people, since their ancestral lands had been taken from them and they had been denied the right to speak their own language and so were deprived of all the cultural memories that it held. In order to survive, they either found low-paid work in farming communities or they lived within the poverty of the townships.

The British first claimed the Cape in 1620 and the Dutch East India Company colonised it in 1652. The British made a second claim in 1806 and in the conflicts that followed many Dutch Boers, or Trekboers – travelling farmers – as they were often called, began pushing further and further north to escape from British control and to find a new life for themselves. Once they had been given access to land grants in the 1830s, they moved like locusts, driving their cattle and their fat-tailed sheep further and further into the Karoo and giving their names to farms which they could now call their own.

All that a Trekboer needed in order to begin a new life was an old wagon and a span of ten oxen to pull it, a horse and two mares, around fifty cows and young cattle, and perhaps five hundred sheep. Within the wagon there would be a gun and a good supply of ammunition, an axe, an adze, a hammer, a couple of storage chests, a Bible – but no other books – a butter churn, a large iron pot for boiling soap and one or two smaller pots for cooking. And a wife of course, and perhaps he already had quite a few children with the hope of more to come. Before setting out he would have hired a family of so-called Hottentots who could do the herding work, since they were a cattle-herding people.

Groups of Trekboers would often combine forces for safety's sake and then, hey presto, off they went into the wilderness, in search of water and pasturage. They lived mostly on meat: freshly killed game cooked over an open fire and strips of dried meat, known as biltong, which was eaten instead of bread. They would also have dried maize and a good supply of spirits and tobacco.

They seemed to have been a strangely wild and savage people, in spite of, or maybe because of, their strict religious beliefs.

As soon as they had found a suitable area they erected crude shelters made out of animal skins and branches, and if it proved fertile enough for longer-term occupation they might build *corbelles*, domed structures like large bread ovens, made of mud bricks. An area of fourteen miles by fourteen could probably support one family, a few helpers, the cattle and the sheep.

> . . . and so it is that the cattle go down to the water and the cattle drink, and the cattle drink and the cattle drink drink drink drink drink, the cattle drink, filling the cattle. And the cattle come out of the water while the cattle go to the grass. And the cattle reach the grass; and the cattle eat it; and the cattle fill themselves with grass, in the morning. (//Kabbo)

The Trekboers did not understand the fragile nature of the land in which they found themselves. In their desire for water, they diverted the rivers during the rainy season in order to grow a bit of grain, but this released crystallised salt particles into the soil, quickly turning it saline and useless. In order to have a steady supply of drinking water for the livestock, they fenced in waterholes and dammed up springs and briefly flowing rivers with earthen walls, but during a rainstorm these walls were easily broken, causing a rush of water that took the topsoil away.

Once the damage was done, they moved on in search of another place; the sad lowing and bleating of their animals carried on the wind, the signs of their passing shown in the trampling of sharp hooves that cut through the delicate plants of the veld, while the fierce hunger of these beasts that did not belong within the hierarchy of life in the Karoo caused them to indiscriminately tear up anything that might be edible.

And so they pushed further into the interior and into /Xam territories, and every time they found a source of water they claimed it as their own, closing it off from the people to whom it had belonged for all the generations that came before.

> . . . the water tastes bitter because it is not new water. It is our father's water. He grew up by it. He lived by it. Our father's father when he died, he left the water to our father. Our father has grown old. Dying, he will leave me the water and I must take it. (//Kabbo)

I suppose the Trekboers were afraid in surroundings that were so unfamiliar and dangerous, when all they had to protect themselves was the power of their guns and a resolute belief that they were entering what they called the *bedoelde land*, the land that God meant them to have, even if that involved taking it from others. They often justified themselves with words from the Old Testament, especially the Psalms.

> I shall give thee the heathen for thine inheritance and the uttermost parts of the earth for thine possession. Thou shalt break them with a rod of iron; thou shalt dash them in pieces like a potter's vessel. (Psalm 2: 8–9)

> Every beast of the forest is mine . . . all the fowls of the mountains and the wild beasts of the field are mine . . . for the world is mine. And the fullness thereof. (Psalm 50: 10–12)

Because of the fear, combined with a sense of entitlement, the Trekboers described every living thing that was not in some way useful or obedient to them as *ongediert*, which translates as vermin. Eland and giraffe, springbok and lion, hyena and ostrich were vermin; the milder ones blamed for drinking the water and competing for the vegetation, while the fiercer ones would kill the livestock and even the owners of the livestock, given half a chance. Kill or be killed.

> The springbok resembles the water of the sea. The spring-bok come in numbers to this place, they cover this place. Therefore the gunpowder of the Boers grows tired, the bullets (shots, balls) of the Boers grow tired. (/Han‡kass'o)

The people of the place, the /Xam whose language was said to be as meaningless as the chatter of birds and whose way of life was said to place them on the lowest rung of humanity, were also looked upon as vermin and 'exterminated on contact'. They had been denied access to water, the animals they relied on for food were disappearing at a terrible speed and it was a crime to kill a sheep or a bullock. Many of the /Xam were shot and in some places the massacre of several hundred was recorded; others died of starvation or from the punishments they received for stock theft. Lucy Lloyd's notebooks are filled with memories of hunger and murder.

> Our fathers taught us we must ourselves feed ourselves and not think that other people, people who are different to us, would be those to give us food. (Dia!kwain)

> Mmei !ka killed along with his father in a fight with the Boers.
> !Kkwai ttu, a girl, taken by the Boers, when her father was killed by the Boers.
> Yarri kkumm (Ostrich Talk) . . . who married //Go (Great Tortoise) . . . who was killed soon after the marriage in the general slaughter by the Boers.

//Kwi // //khwi ka tin who was killed with his father as a little boy, by the Boers.

Xwain who married ‡Nou !kiou, son of !Xauko and of ‡Xi, who was killed by the Boers in a fight over cattle, his widow dying later at her son's place.

VI

12 April 2020. When I came home I had fourteen days in lock-down to see if I had caught the virus on the crowded plane. The man who lolled his head on my shoulder had not worried me. But in the tight confinement of economy class there was a young man in the seat in front of me who kept moving about, standing up and sitting down, and when he turned and I saw his face it was flushed and wet with the sweat of a fever. Not knowing what else to do I put the British Airways red brushed-nylon blanket over my head and closed my eyes. But he carried nothing, or at least I caught nothing from him, unless the tickling cough and the vague headache were a version of what he had.

I have been told how painful the process of dying will be if I am claimed by this tiny enemy that wears so many crowns. I am sure it might be true, but I keep reassuring myself with the words of the French philosopher Montaigne. He was terrified of the idea of death and the pain of it, until the day when he was knocked violently from his horse and no one thought he would live. 'My soul,' he said, 'hung from my lip,' as it observed from a distance the strange spectacle of his damaged and helpless body. I hope my soul, or something like it, will also know how to hang from my lip, if need be.

I need to lean on the solace of such a thought. The weather

has turned winter-cold, the wind is sharp, my two marrow plants have given up the ghost and are brown and withered, and my courage keeps tumbling out of me. I remember reading somewhere that when David Livingstone was attacked by a lion, he said he was overwhelmed by what he called a 'great lassitude' and also felt no pain or fear. Of course there was the initial shock and the meaty stink of the creature's breath as it opened its mouth to bite into him, but the recollection of the lassitude was what remained. It makes sense, or at least it does at this moment.

> The man turned his head a little and the lion wondered why the man's head moved. It pressed the man's head more firmly between the branches of the tree. The man cried quietly because he saw himself in the lion's paws and in great danger and wept on account of it and the lion licked the man's eyes. (Dia!kwain)

My mind turns to another lion. A friend was sexually abused by his father who worked as a lion tamer in a circus. After many years the friend summoned up the courage to invite his father to come and see him, to talk about the crimes he had committed, and the father agreed, but said he would do just one more show before setting off. The lion must have felt the man's terror, or perhaps it felt the weight of his guilt, because it killed him, there in the ring. My husband and I were sitting at a table in the moonlight on the terrace of our house in Italy in a time that now feels like a lifetime ago, and because of the intimacy of the glimmering darkness, as we listened to our friend's story it seemed to unfold before our eyes.

> The lion walking at night . . . steals up to the hut that it may kill a person. It snatches up the person and runs into the night's blackness. (Dia!kwain)

The /Xam were respectful and afraid of the lion; they saw him as an equal in power and authority, and there was always the possibility of the lion becoming the man, the woman becoming the lioness.

Our mother ordered her children to never call out when they were alone in the veld. Our mother told us that a lion who wanted to resemble a person puts his tail in his mouth and calls out to us, sounding like a man. That is why we must not answer if we hear a thing calling to us there, for we feel it is a lion that wants to resemble a man to us . . . The lions used to be very numerous in the Bushmen's country, but are so no longer. (Dia!kwain)

My aunt used to turn herself into a lioness. She sought for us. She wanted to see whether we were still comfortable where we lived . . . She roared like a lioness because she wished that we should hear her, that we should know it was she who had come seeking us. (Dia!kwain)

This is a story about a woman who was called a Lion's Woman, because she knew how to make the step from the one body to the other:

A woman is travelling with a man. The woman carries the child. They see quagga.
The man says, 'I am hungry.' He says to the woman, 'Make yourself into a lion, so we may catch quagga and eat.'
The woman says he will be afraid if she is a lion. The man says he will not be afraid.
The woman becomes a lion. Her hair becomes a lion's hair, her claws become the lion's claws, her face becomes the lion's face. She lays the child upon the ground.

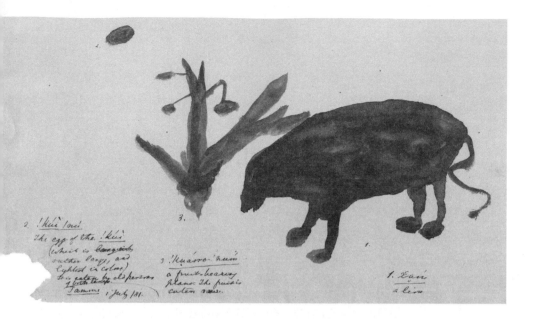

The man is afraid, he climbs into a tree.

The woman looks at him. She runs to the side of the path. She takes off her skin garment. She becomes a lion.

The woman goes into the bushes. She creeps up on the quagga, she jumps on the quagga, she kills it, she drinks the blood.

The lion comes back to the child that cries.

The man in the tree calls out, 'Put off the lion's skin! Make yourself into a woman!'

The lion growls. The lion looks at the man who cannot come down from the tree while the woman is a lion.

Disappear the lion! Disappear the lion's mane! Disappear the lion's tail!

The woman puts off the lion. She puts on her garment of skin. She becomes a woman. She takes up the child.

The man comes down from the tree. They eat quagga, he and the woman. (Hottentot legend translated by /A!kunta)

39

VII

18 April 2020. Before I went to the Karoo I kept getting stuck. I had lots of books to refer to and I used them to write several chapters, but the chapters were no good and I threw them out. I spent ages trying to describe the kind of person I was when I first came across the /Xam texts in *Specimens of Bushman Folklore* and why I was so drawn to them, but I threw those chapters out too. I felt I had to set the scene of how the interviews with the /Xam were put together and that seemed to mean providing a detailed account of the man who started the work of making the archive and the woman who helped him with it – where they were born, what they looked like and how their task evolved over the years – but they appeared like a distraction from the main story and so those chapters had to go as well.

In the end all that was really left from more than a year of work was page after page of short excerpts I had copied from Bleek and Lloyd's book, from later anthropological studies, and from a complete transcript of the original notebooks, which had been put together in 2012 by a young man called Mark McGranaghan, when he was working on his PhD thesis for Oxford University. Early in 2018, I had arranged to meet Mark at the British Library, and he pinged the transcript to me, all 12,000 notebook pages of it. I would drift through the dense, repetitive and often very complicated sequences of what was being said, sometimes pausing to turn a sentence into a little poem and then back into a slightly edited version of itself and then back again to its original form. As I repeated this process, the voices of strangers from another time began to lodge themselves in my mind.

My mother does not eat. She lies down with hunger. She wants to say she is there. She does not eat, she is hungry, while she speaks, she is there. (/A!kunta)

I kept returning to these texts, trawling through them to try to catch anything I had missed or forgotten. Slowly the people who were speaking became more familiar to me and their way of thinking and seeing now gives me a sort of courage in the curiously locked-down state that I am in and we are all in.

I realise that what I need to do is to try to give the view from the other side; to try to enter a sense of the nature of the universe in which the /Xam lived, in order to understand what it must have been like to be invaded by my lot, the whites, with our guns, our presumptions and our cruelty, as we moved like a plague through unexplored regions, claiming everything as our own and leaving a trail of destruction in our wake.

We, these new invaders, so utterly different to any other living creature the /Xam had encountered. It was not just the suddenness of our arrival out of nowhere, the deathly white or hot pink of whatever parts of our skin were made visible. It was not just our wagons and snorting trains that seemed like great beasts, or our railway lines and roads and fences that shut off the freedom of old paths and tracks forever. It was not even the unlimited possessions that came to us in boxes and crates; the heavy chains to bind our prisoners, the whips to punish them, the increasingly efficient guns that could kill from a safe distance. All these things were powerful and frightening, but what was far more shocking about us was surely our utter indifference to the land we had entered and to the variations of life in its many forms that the land held and fostered.

The face of the country was literally white with spring-bok . . . pouring down like locusts from the endless plains . . . When hunted, these elegant creatures take extraordinary bounds, rising with curved backs high in the air as if about to take flight. (Captain W. C. Harris, 1836 and 1837)

It almost exceeds belief how many black rhinoceros daily exhibit themselves . . . its attacks, although sudden and impetuous, are easily eluded and a shot behind the shoulder from the distance of twenty or thirty yards, generally proves fatal. (Harris)

There could have been no fewer than three hundred elephants within the scope of our vision . . . they all proved to be ladies and most of them mothers, followed by their little old-fashioned calves . . . eventually both wagons were so crammed with spolia, that, being unable to find room for any more ivory, we were reluctantly compelled to leave the ground strewed with that valuable commodity. (Harris)

Equus Quagga, formerly so numerous on the Karoo plains, has become extinct. It was a fine strong animal, more horse-like than the zebra and from the little evidence obtainable, more amenable to domestication. (H. A. Bryden, 1889)

The mole rats are curious animals, with long exposed incisor teeth, powerful claws for burrowing and exceedingly small eyes. Their fur is remarkably soft and dense and would doubtless be valuable commercially in the making of top hats . . . if collected in sufficient quantities. (Bryden)

The /Xam did not feel the need to have mastery or ownership. For them everything was equally alive, equally important.

Quaggas weep if another quagga is wounded. They cry and make a noise together if they smell the scent of blood. (Dia!kwain)

'I'he gemsbok understands. He sits in the tree's shade. He watching sits. He turns his ears towards his back to listen. He smells watching the man. He sits, the wind blowing behind him. 'I understand and listen,' he says. (//Kabbo)

They were absorbed in a continuous conversation not only with living creatures in the present, but also with those same creatures as they were in the time of the Early Race when all things were people, not just the lion and the praying mantis, but also the Moon and the Stars, the Wind and the Rain.

The Moon walks, holding up his head. He walks singing . . . he seems alive because he sees with his eyes. He sees the clouds because his eyes are alive. He goes leaping into the clouds. (//Kabbo)

The Rain carries off a young girl. She becomes a flower that grows, standing in the water. We see the flowers. They are beautiful but we do not pick them, because they are the girls the Rain has taken, they are the water's wives. (//Kabbo)

The intimate connection with everything that surrounded them made it possible for the people to ignore the confinement of their own bodies. The woman becomes the lion. The dancer becomes the animal which is represented in the dance. The hunter becomes his prey. Someone who enters a trance state needs to die in order to make the difficult journey into the land of the dead to learn things there, before returning to the land of the living. And for their part, the dead are everywhere, close to the living.

> Grandfather turned himself into a jackal. He walked with us as a jackal. At other times, grandfather turns himself into a little bird. He comes to where we live. He flies above our heads. He sits looking at us, to see if we are different and what has happened to us since he left. He seems to listen when we speak to him. When he has heard us say we are not ill, he flies away. (Dia!kwain)

The people were also able to step across the barriers that divide the past from the present. You think of a place as it once was and you enter that place, even if it belongs to another time than your own. You think of the First at Sitting People, the ones who lifted the sun into the sky so that the world became light and you are there among them. When you see a praying mantis no bigger than your hand, you also see him in the shape of /Kaggen, an old man of the Early Race, who gave the colours to the hartebeest, the gemsbok, the springbok and the eland and named the places in the /Xam-ka !au lands and created the moon when he threw a shoe into the sky. And when you see a lion walking across the red sand of the Karoo, you see the first lion from that other time.

> He is a lion who talks, he eats people, he talks. He is a lion, he is a man, he has hair, he is a lion, his hands are a man's hands. (//Kabbo)

As I read a these texts I seem to be grabbing at the tail of a memory that escapes from me even as I reach out to catch hold of it. We have learned to be confined within the span of a single life and within the experience of a single body, and yet we are haunted by the sense of having lost a state of being in which it was possible to know what it means to be something other than ourselves, whether that other is a fellow human, an animal, a tree, or the full moon looking down at the earth from the sky.

The lion says, 'I lie on my back to cool my stomach, for the ground is cool. The wind blows on my stomach as I lie on my back. I walk to the water. I stand by the edge of the water and I drink as I stand, I drink so my stomach is full. I feel that I am a great lion, my thinking strings speak in this manner to me. (//Kabbo)

It seemed as if the wind cried with her when her tears fell. Then the wind did not want her tears to fall, for it was not willing that she should cry, for the wind used to blow whenever she cried, because the wind did not want the tears from her eyes to fall. (Dia!kwain)

When the people see a star that has fallen they say, 'we shall bear the news, for the star tells us a bad thing has happened in another place.' (Dia!kwain)

I resemble my father hyena. My face resembles my father's face. My eyes resemble my father's eyes. My hair resembles my father's hair. We are all black. Our head hair is short. Our heads are big. (/A!kunta)

The baboon is a thing that does not want to die. For it knows what is coming. It knows when death threatens. (/Han‡kass'o)

To a people like the /Xam we must have appeared as creatures that lacked something crucial in our nature; creatures who did not seem to understand pity:

> We shall see whether we make those people cry as we
> do, for they do not seem to know that we are people.
> (Dia!kwain)

We apparently had no sense of the transgression of shooting men, women and children who could not defend themselves; the transgression of shooting thousands of migrating springbok as they moved forward like a great river; the transgression of leaving baby elephants abandoned beside the bodies of their mothers because of a growing demand for that stuff called ivory, used for billiard balls, crochet hooks and knick-knacks, and for the hundreds of thousands of white keys needed for the growing boom in the sale of upright pianos. And it seemed that we also had no pity for the land itself, but were willing to casually tear it apart, change it beyond all recognition, or even destroy it entirely.

And now the pandemic moves among us and we do not know what to do with our fear and our sense of culpability in the face of it; how to save ourselves in a world we thought we owned, to do with it as we wished.

VIII

20 April 2020, and I mourn a third friend who has died from corona. I did not know that he was ill and in hospital and for two weeks after his death I did not know that he was dead, and that has left me with a particular sense of desolation. I wish I had been given some sort of a sign to prepare me for the loss.

A presentiment is a thing we feel when something is happening in another place. It is like a dream which we dream. Sometimes when we are alone our body is startled, it seems as if something were there which our body feared . . . with the tapping we feel the things to come. (Dia!kwain)

We feel in our bodies that certain things are going to happen . . . when an ostrich is coming and scratching the back of its neck with its foot, the Bushman feels the tapping in the lower part of his own neck at the same place where the ostrich is scratching . . . The springbok when coming scratches itself with its horns and with its foot and then the Bushman feels the tapping. When a woman who had gone is returning to the house, the man who is sitting there feels on his shoulder the thong with which the woman's child is slung over her shoulders, he feels the tapping there.

He feels the rustling of the feet of the springbok when the springbok comes, making the bushes rustle. He has a sensation on his face, on account of the blackness of the stripe on the face of the springbok. He has a sensation in his eyes, on account of the black marks around the eyes of the springbok.

Ever since I first read *Specimens of Bushman Folklore* all those years ago, I have returned again and again to //Kabbo's description of the tapping sensation and the dream of closeness that he says we can dream, which allows us to step over the barrier that separates us from each other and from the future and the past. I think I have used it as a sort of guide.

I'll try to explain. New York and as part of my research into the life of the singer Billie Holiday, my husband and I were staying in an old boarding house in Harlem. A single manacle from a pair of handcuffs was locked onto the handrail of the carved mahogany banister that curled its way up to the top floor where we had a room. In that room a mouse was racing in circles in the wastepaper basket and the very battered double bed in which we were to sleep had one side worn into a cradled dip, as if countless men and women had been sitting there over the years, head in hands, wondering what to do, how to manage in a world that gave them no dignity, no room to breathe. And for a moment it was as if Billie Holiday was also there and I could feel her exhaustion, her desperation in the face of the racism that threatened every aspect of her life; a predicament that she could only transcend with the power of her singing.

When I was writing about the Spanish painter Goya as an old man on the edge of life but unafraid of the fact of death, I was also caring for my mother who was on that same edge and equally calm in her manner of being, and sometimes it was as if the two of them were one and the same person, joined by the shared experience of imminent mortality.

In Australia's Great Western Desert, I was sitting on the ground next to a woman called May, ochre-red waves of sandhills stretching out on all sides of us and into a far distance, and for the short time that I sat there with her it was as if I were a member of her family and could see that red land with her eyes and with her longing for a way of life that had been swept away when she was still a child.

Just before I left for Cape Town, Elrina, who was born on the farm close to the spring known as Bitterpits where //Kabbo and his family had lived for so many generations, sent me a photograph of the landscape around her house. The sky was streaked in the pale blue and pink and soft yellow light of the setting sun, and beneath the sky lay a flat and golden-brown expanse of land stretching out into the distance. In the foreground I could distinguish tiny stones like seeds, among bigger stones in different colours, while on the far horizon there was an undulating shape that I thought was a gathering of clouds, although in fact these were the low hills where the volcanic boulders lie, but I did not know that then. The photograph brought me hurtling back to a time when I was stuck in my writing work and stuck in all sorts of other ways as well, my neck and shoulders aching from carrying the weight of my head and my head aching from carrying the weight of so many fears about so many things. I went to visit a healer and sat in a chair facing a window that looked towards a meadow where a horse was grazing, but I had my eyes closed and so I saw nothing, and as I sat there I watched a swaying line of people approaching me across a shimmering desert and they were singing even though I could not hear their voices, and with that I was comforted. And now, so many years later, when I expanded Elrina's photograph on my mobile I seemed to be looking at the same landscape where I had seen the line of people.

In Cape Town, before I set off to the Karoo and //Kabbo's place, Tanya took me to a market of street sellers. It was chaotic and friendly and disquieting as well because we were just becoming aware of the coronavirus moving like a wind around the world, turning strangers into threatening presences. I stopped at a stall selling paintings on pieces of thin cloth heaped on the pavement like piles of fruit and I picked up a flimsy painting no bigger than three postcards in a row. It showed a swaying line of people moving towards me across a flat landscape, and in that moment of recognition I bought it and now I have it pinned on the wall facing my desk and I can almost hear the people singing.

Oh old woman! At what place did you grow up? You will speak to me the place's name, the place where you did grow up. You shall tell me the place at which you did grow up; the place from which you come from; the place where you seemed to live, when you were a child.

. . . and you must tell me the names of your people, your father's name and your mother's name and you must also speak the names of your children.

And you must speak your name, the thing which your name seems to be like. And you must speak your Bushman name, the name which your parents spoke. That is the name you must speak. And afterwards you must speak your European name.

Then I shall be able to hear from what you say, whether you are of Bushman, whether you speak Bushman . . . You must also speak Bushman language, so I shall be able to hear if you sound like me . . . (Dia!kwain)

IX

22 April 2020. The chicken wire arrived. It was shorter and lower and more flimsy than I had expected, but never mind. Because I had no posts to hold it firm I draped it around a clump of bushes and a lilac tree and performed all sorts of complicated hammerings and fixings and weighing downs, banging my thumbnail and lacerating the side of my index finger in the process. But now the chickens are here and safe and they have a rather cramped wooden house with two nesting boxes, although it will probably be a while before they think of laying an egg. I have placed a red metal chair within the enclosure, so I can sit among them if I want to.

The next day was difficult. I managed to get a tiny smear of the sticky stuff from the plaster that covered the cut on my finger onto my hard contact lenses and I couldn't clean them, no matter how much I tried. Without the lenses, the world becomes distant. With the spectacles I rarely use, it becomes so sharply defined that I feel I might lose my balance within it. So I kept wearing the dirty lenses, but I was seeing everything through a mist and the mist somehow enveloped me and allowed a panic to move in and take up occupation. I suppose an edge of fear is always somewhere close by in this locked-down time, but mostly I keep it at bay.

Darkness resembles fear. When trees do not stand in brightness, people are afraid of the trees. They are afraid of the trees that have darkness in themselves. (‡Kasin)

Eventually I got the lenses clean, but the fear would not leave me and so I drove to the nearest stretch of the coast and walked very fast towards the sea, following a path through silver birch woods, the trees floating in pools of sunlight, not yet obscured by young leaves. Two buzzards were mewing like cats in the sky. I stooped to pick up a peacock butterfly that looked dead, but it shuddered into life. I knew the path very well, but it seemed to unroll itself with infinite slowness.

The grey sea when I reached it was somehow unforgiving and indifferent, but it was good to sit on the shore and stare at it until I hardly felt myself to be there and staring. That night I fell asleep quite easily but I woke in the dark before the dawn with the last vestiges of fear still fluttering around my head. I went out into the cold garden and climbed the steps to the upper level of what was once a steep-sided sandpit and crouched down in front of eight runner bean plants which I had recently planted and wrapped a plastic bag around each one to protect it from the frost I felt might come and kill them. With that my own fear had gone and I slept through until the morning.

So now it's 25 April and I think I am ready to begin the story of how a group of /Xam were brought to Cape Town.

They were captured in the last months of 1869 or early in 1870 as part of what was known as a 'mopping up operation' in the northern Karoo. They were accused of cattle rustling which probably meant that they and their families had eaten part of a sheep or a bullock they had managed to kill, or had found already dead. The punishment for such a crime was imprisonment and something in the region of two years' hard labour. The women and children were punished by default, since their husbands and fathers, sons, brothers and uncles were taken away, leaving them destitute and with even less of a chance of survival.

> I shall drink the water. I am hungry. He sits. He cannot speak for hunger. He cannot stand up for hunger. One ox is white. One ox is red. You kill the lion and the leopard and the lion and the leopard kill the two of us. (Adam Kleinhardt)

Sometimes children under the age of eight were taken and 'tamed' so they could be used as servants.

> !gam ke ǂei yang e hin //hion ka xoro: The Bushmen eat the cattle of the Boers.
> //hung an /keye ge hin //hion yan /hanken: The Boers take the children of the Bushmen. (Adam Kleinhardt)

The arrests of the men had a useful and practical purpose. There were new roads and railway lines to be built in the expanding territory of the Cape Province and a breakwater was being constructed in the Cape Town harbour, in order to make it safe for an increasing number of ships to dock there. The prison which supplied the labour force was aptly named the Breakwater Jail. It stood close to a stone quarry and just above the Table Bay, where the rocks needed to be deposited.

The man called Oude Jantje Tooren by the Boers, but //Kabbo by his people, told the story. He must have been born around 1815. He had three /Xam names: /Uhi-ddoro, or Smoking Tinderbox, //Kabbo, which means Dream, while his 'little name', given to him as a baby, was /Hanǂiǂi, or Husband's Thoughts, perhaps because he was the youngest of six children and his father had a late desire for his mother.

> Koi-ang is the name of my mother. I cannot remember the names of my father, or my brother, they died when I was a

child. An old Bushman whose hair was very white took care of me. His name, given to him by the Boers, was Old Bastard and his Bushman name was ‡Kua/hai. (//Kabbo)

I have been looking up the meanings of some of the Afrikaans names given to the Bushmen. I speak Dutch, but for this I needed to find the words in an Afrikaans dictionary, given to me by Peter, the second of my friends who died of corona. Oude Jantje Tooren means Old Johnny Juggler or Witchcraft Maker. His son, //Goo-ka-!kui or Smoke's Man, was known as Witbooi, Whiteboy, presumably because he had a pale skin colour; another man was Little Toe, and a woman was called Oude Lies, which could mean Old Groin, although, to be fair, Lies is also a girl's name. Finally, /A!kunta was known as Klaas Stoffel, a word that means idiot, or blockhead.

Anyway, on we go: //Kabbo was with his family in the little gathering of round huts where they lived at a bit of a distance from the Bitterpits waterhole, which they knew by its ancestral name of //Xare-//kam. The distance was maintained so as not to disturb the animals that came there to drink. As he says:

There is my wife, there am I, there is my son's wife, there is my daughter, she carries a child who is very small, there is my daughter's husband. We are few. It was so. (//Kabbo)

Like all of their people, they were hungry, but on that day //Kabbo had shot a springbok with an arrow and they were about to eat it. Maybe they had also killed a sheep or a bullock or found one that was dead, since livestock theft was the crime they were accused of, but if so, he doesn't mention it.

Policemen came. They bound //Kabbo's arms and they bound the arms of his brother-in-law /Han‡kass'o and the arms of his son //Goo-ka-!kui who was Witbooi to the Boers. They were dressed to look like farmhands and they were put into the wagon.

Their women tried to join them in the wagon but were pushed away and so they followed on foot as best they could.

The wagon stopped for the first night. The women arrived and made a fire and Witbooi's wife was carrying the springbok meat which they roasted over the fire. They smoked tobacco before lying down to sleep.

When the day broke they again made a fire and smoked tobacco. But now the men were 'tied to the wagon's chain' and had to run alongside of it.

They arrived at Victoria West, a little town which had a church, a town hall, a shop with provisions for the scattered sheep farmers and a prison. //Kabbo was brought before a doctor.

> The doctor asked the other white man for my name. He said, 'What is the name of that man there?' 'I am //Kabbo! I am //Kabbo!' I said to the other white man. The other man goes away.

The three men were tried by the magistrate, Maximilian Jackson. They were each charged with cattle rustling and sentenced to two years' hard labour. They were put in the jail, their legs held in wooden stocks.

> We are taken to the jail's house in the dark. We put our legs to the wood and another white man laid other wood upon our legs. We sleep while our legs are in the wood. The day breaks while our legs are in the wood. While it is early we take our legs out of the wood and eat meat. We again put our legs to the wood and sit. We again lie down. We sleep while our legs are in the wood. We wake, we smoke, the people cook sheep's flesh while our legs are in the wood.
>
> We rolled the stones at Victoria. We carried the stones on our breasts. We rolled great stones. We worked the ground. We carried the earth. We filled the wagons with

earth. We pushed it. We pushed the wagons' wheels. We pushed. We threw out the earth. Again they tied our arms to the wagon chain.

They remained in Victoria West for almost four months and the women managed to join them there after a journey of some 150 kilometres. But when the men were moved on to the town of Beaufort West the women could not keep up with them.

We came to Beaufort while the sun was hot, We came into Beaufort Jail. Early the next morning our arms were made fast, we were bound to the wagons. We splashed into the water. We splashed, passing through the water in the river-bed. We walked, being bound, until we, being bound, came to the Breakwater Jail. We came and worked at it.

So now they were in Cape Town and this jail was their final destination. It had a reputation for being overcrowded and brutal, 'for human misery I suppose there has never been anything in South Africa to match it'. The prisoners were sent out every day in chain gangs, to work at the quarry face to provide stones for the Breakwater harbour or to work on the construction of railway cuttings, mountain passes and roads. Any minor disobedience was severely punished: one man was given three days' solitary confinement for being noisy on a Sunday; another got two days for not washing his trousers at the proper time. A much heavier punishment was the treadmill, a device with no purpose beyond that of keeping a man walking with effort and without a pause, and if he tired just for a moment, then the machine hacked mercilessly at his shins.

//Kabbo was older than most of his fellow prisoners. He was estimated to be in his mid-fifties, and according to something called the Descriptions Register of the Breakwater Jail, he was four feet nine inches tall, had a wart on the left side of his brow and, like many /Xam hunters, the top joint of both his little fingers had been removed.

The Register provides a very specific description of him, as prisoner No. 4:

Pure Yellow Bushman
Head: bullet headed (spherical skull)
Skin: tawny yellow in colour, much wrinkled
Hair: small tufts of crinkly hair, sparsely scattered over scalp
Face: plain and Simian type
Eyes: deeply set
Chin: small or absent
Cheek bones: prominent
Lips: everted [meaning pushed outwards, as opposed to inverted]
Expression: inscrutable
Hands: small
Feet: small.

There are also four photographs of him, taken at the prison on 31 January 1871 as part of a research project initiated by Thomas Huxley, the president of the newly formed Anthropological Society in London. Huxley was keen 'to obtain photographs from the various Colonies . . . as illustrating the peculiarities of the various Races within the British Possessions', and apparently Wilhelm Bleek was interested in the idea of adding these researches to his own and happy to help.

According to Huxley's detailed instructions, each subject had to be photographed naked, in full-body and seated upper-body postures, both full face and in profile, with a measuring rod alongside the body, so that the relevant data could be easily obtained. When standing they were to hold the right arm outstretched and the left arm along the side of the body. The positioning of the head, feet and hands was also carefully specified: the feet close together 'in an attitude of attention', the left hand flat against the upper thigh.

//Kabbo was photographed in this way, in the name of modern science. He sits facing the camera, staring into its glinting eye. He sits in profile. He stands naked, holding a measuring stick. He stands naked in profile, holding the measuring stick out at an angle from his body. The look of detachment is not once altered as the camera does its work, but perhaps detachment is the wrong word.

//Kabbo appears serious, sombre, intense and far away from his present predicament. He is enduring what is happening to him from some private distance. Maybe like Montaigne who observed himself lying wounded on the ground, //Kabbo observed himself trapped in a prison from which he could not escape, and for him, too, his soul hung from his lip.

X

I have been watching a woman called Elsie Vaalbooi in a film called *Tracks across Sand*. She was from another Bushman group known as the //Khomani who had always lived on the edge of the red sands of the Kalahari Desert, but in recent times she and her people had been moved to a township in the Northern Cape and that was where she was being interviewed.

In the film Elsie was 102, which means that when she died in 2002, she had reached the age of 105. She sits in a chair outside a rough corrugated hut. She wears a flowery dress. The skin of her face is pale and blotched with the marks and freckles of her age. The skin is limp rather than lined and it looks as if it would be very soft to the touch. Her mouth is full and rather loose in its movements in the way that the mouth of an old person can be. One eye is almost shut, the other eye is wide open and surprisingly large: it drifts slightly in its gaze, so maybe the focus is not so good.

Elsie was at first thought to be the only person alive who could still understand N'uu and she is asked to listen to a recording of a N'uu speaker from the 1930s. A crackling voice is playing and she is lost in concentration. When the voice stops, she says in Afrikaans:

My language is my first husband who disappeared. After all these years I see him again and he does not know what

I want. I am so nervous I can hardly speak to him, but I have to speak to him because he took the trouble to return to me. I am happy to see him and greet him, but I cannot speak any more. I am old. I will speak a little to him when I am alone, when I can catch my breath. What he asks of me, appeals to me, but I am very tired. I have suffered a lot, but after all I am still myself. I am still the same old Elsie Vaalbooi.

The film-makers learn there might be other N'uu speakers in another run-down settlement in this part of the Northern Cape. They find Antje, shy and very feminine in spite of her extreme old age. She listens to the same recording and a little smile of recognition flickers across her face. 'Do you understand?' someone asks. 'Yes,' she replies, 'the girl is saying, "Where are the bones? You said you brought the bones!"'

A second woman has come to sit with Antje. They start talking of the past. 'You washed yourself with the pulp from a melon. You washed your arms, your legs, your belly.' And as they talk, they smile and rub their old hands on the young and naked arms and legs and bellies that they can suddenly feel under their clothed bodies.

In another of these almost derelict townships – corrugated-iron shacks, doors made from sacking, chickens and thin children milling about in the dust – three sisters are sitting in a row on three chairs. They have very sculpted faces: high cheekbones, wide-set eyes, pale skin. They wear brightly coloured scarves wound around their heads and a mishmash of bright jewellery. They laugh a lot, covering the mouth with an elegant hand when they do.

Asked about their language, one of the sisters says, 'I did not discard my mother tongue, but the children do not understand it. They say it sounds like birds.'

A second sister says, 'We buried our language,' and she leans forward and with her finger she draws a little trench into the soft sand at her feet. 'We hid it,' she says and she takes a few pinches of the sand and sprinkles them into the trench as if she were scattering seeds. She covers the language over with a gentle sweeping movement and pats it down. 'We made it hidden until it could return.'

The three of them have always had each other to talk to, quietly, secretly. 'Our parents would go early and fetch some melon and return at night and make a small amount of porridge. We would eat and become full. We would lie down. That was how we lived. We did not live by eating bread. We did not know bread. We drank tea of the acacia tree. The acacia trees were there, on that side,' and they look towards the place from where the acacias have gone.

The sisters listen to the same recording from the 1930s. There is something about an old man who wants to marry a young girl but she will not have him. And then here comes the bone. 'The bone the man is talking about is the rib of the gemsbok antelope. It must not be eaten. It must be set aside. Now it is time for the maiden to step out of the hut. And when she steps out of the hut she paints her face like this, with a red stone that makes her face shine. And when she steps out they roast the gemsbok rib.'

With that the three old women clap their hands in the rhythm of a song, and their thin high voices sing of the maiden who has become a woman. It is as if they are back where they once were. A fire is burning, people are dancing, their bare feet as light as the feet of antelopes as they lift them and let them drop on the soft ground.

The film moves to the face of a man sitting close by. He says he cannot speak the N'uu language, but he can understand it. He says it is his food. He says the Boers hated a person who spoke the Bushman language. 'They called the Bushmen dogs. They herded us in a heap. We became afraid. That is when the language took flight, when the Boer came with his thick voice. We had to speak Afrikaans to him and he would shoot us down. In those days we

could not be together. We had to scatter. We had to dip down, dip down and scatter . . .'

I just now had an email from Janette Deacon. She is the archaeologist who organised my trip to the Karoo. She is in her early eighties and first went there in 1985, searching for the places spoken of by /A!kunta and //Kabbo, /Han‡kass'o and Dia!kwain and the others. Since then she has steadfastly continued her studies.

The landscapes survive, even though they have been altered almost beyond recognition, and the /Xam language survives in a way, along with an understanding of the world that the language encompassed, thanks to the notebook pages in the Bleek and Lloyd Archive. But like the //Khomani, the people themselves were forbidden to communicate in /Xam because that would have allowed them to remember a time before the arrival of the whites, a time in which they had a different sense of power and identity. It was thought that the last of the speakers had died out by the beginning of the twentieth century, but in 1985 Janette was told of a ninety-year-old man called Abraham Barend who lived in the Bushmanland region, in the village of Swartkop – which means black head or hill in Afrikaans. He had been a child of Bushmen parents at the turn of the twentieth century. The language he spoke was Nama not /Xam, but he was knowledgeable about indigenous plant foods and medicine.

Janette visited the farm where Abraham was living. She took a photograph of him wearing a dirty jacket that overwhelmed his small, thin frame and in the photo he looks timid and fearful. He said his father had been captured by the Boers when he was very young and was kept in a sort of cage, until he had been tamed.

When visiting Abraham, a tape recorder was brought out and set before him and he spoke in Nama, the words which had been lodged in his mind since childhood. 'Quick! We must run away! The Boers are coming!'

Later Janette heard of a very old /Xam speaker called

Hendrik Gould, but he died before she could return to the farm and interview him.

Now, since Abraham's death, there is no one left who can speak /Xam.

Khou/khougen: to think, to remember, to desire, using the 'thinking strings' located on both sides of the front of the neck.

Kamman/kamman: understanding. The notion of understanding was crucial to /Xam interpretation of adult responsibility. It was inculcated through:

Tum: to hear, to listen, to understand, and transmitted in:

Kum: story, talk, history, news.

//Khu//khuken: 'thinking strings. A story enters the ear holes and goes down on each side of the throat and into the thinking strings. It remains there and grows up with the hearer. This story is my mother's mother's story which she told nicely. I got it as it lay on my thinking strings.' (//Kabbo)

XI

In the summer of 2019 I was on a train that kept getting delayed, and because I had a notebook but no book to read I began to entertain myself with words. I wrote about the sunlight flickering on the page and I played with the thought of the screech and squawk from the connecting carriages sounding like an animal in pain. When the train stopped at a station I described the heavy breathing of the engine, the bang of a door like the thud of a hoof followed by a snorting sound as if through wet nostrils.

I then wrote an account of a short sequence from a documentary about the Ju/'hoansi Bushmen of the Kalahari. I had watched it several times and was able to replay it before my eyes like a memory.

The sequence, which lasted for only a few minutes, was made in the 1950s by the American anthropologist John Marshall. His father had been a co-founder of the Raytheon Company which was established in 1922 and became a major US defence contractor and the world's biggest producer of guided missiles – by 2020 the company's profits were more than $54 billion. In 1950 Marshall set off to Namibia with his wife Lorna, their eighteen-year-old son John and their twenty-year-old daughter Elizabeth, in search of the lost world of the Kalahari and the hunter-gatherers who still lived there, by the skin of their teeth you might say.

The Marshalls drove into the Nyae Nyae district in the north-east of Namibia and there they made contact with the Ju/'hoansi. The building up of trust between people of two such very different cultures took a while, but it went well and eventually the Marshalls would come to live within the Ju/'hoansi community on and off for the next ten years or so, sometimes staying for a few months and once for more than a year. Lorna made anthropological field notes and interviewed the people and her first book about them was *The !Kung of Nyae Nyae* (1976). Elizabeth also became a writer and her book *The Harmless People* was published in 1959, while her brother John took very fine photographs and produced hundreds of hours of film on a 16mm camera. Unlike the rest of the family he went on returning to the Ju/'hoansi until the early 1970s when he was expelled by the government for political reasons. He was not able to meet up with the people again until the late 1980s and by that time they had been moved to a settlement called Tsumque and nothing was as it once had been.

In the 1950s John Marshall had followed the men with his film camera as they pursued a giraffe for several days until it crumpled exhausted to the ground and gazed solemnly at the hunters one by one, as if agreeing to its own death. He followed the women and children as they moved lightly through the landscape, collecting seeds and roots, fruit and insects. He filmed people talking and laughing, dancing and silent, old and young, and there was a sense of the joyful energy of simply being alive, although even then it was clear that everything was on the cusp and what W. B. Yeats called 'the centre' could not hold for long. In the sequence that has stayed with me so vividly, Marshall was there to witness a healer as he entered a trance.

The healer must be in his early twenties and his wife is very young, maybe not more than twelve or thirteen. She is as beautiful as a cat and her breasts are just beginning to gather energy, the nipples ripening like dark buds. She has told her husband that she does not want to have sex with him, not yet, and in the film he says this might be why he had become a healer, harnessing the energy of his desire. The camera gazes at his young wife as she rubs her laughing nakedness around the loose and wrinkled body of her old uncle and her uncle laughs with her and without embarrassment.

A woman in the group is heavily pregnant and gravely ill. You see her lying on a leather blanket among the gathering of little huts made of branches and dried grasses. The skin of her face is stretched tight and she is sweating from the fever and from the weight of the baby in her womb. Her eyes are shut, the eyelids flickering as if she is dreaming. A fly keeps settling into the corner of her eyelid to drink its moisture but she does not react. A few children stare at her with vague curiosity but the adults are attentive.

The young man enters a trance and it is as if you are seeing the invisible made briefly visible as you watch him tumbling into another dimension: his mouth open in a funnel of amazement like the mouths of saints in early paintings, when they have been thrown into the presence of their God and there is something like horror as well as wonder in their staring eyes.

He starts to run in a wide circle around the people who are there with him. He runs in smooth loping steps as if he is being blown forward by a wind and an older man follows closely behind him, both of them contained by the precise choreography of their shared movement, two elements within a single body. The older man is there to catch the young man if he falls.

Now the young man has stopped running and he is kneeling beside the woman. He beats the palms of his hands fast and soft on her bare back. He bends forward, his face close to hers as he blows his breath over her, opening the door, or so it would seem, that divides the dead from the living so that she can find a way back.

She stirs as if she is answering his call and with that he

collapses on the ground beside her, his face transfigured by the effort he has made.

The woman lives, but her baby dies. Someone says to John Marshall, 'Your questions about death are senseless. It is just the way things are.'

There is another sequence that I have also watched several times. It was made when John Marshall was finally given permission to return to Nyae Nyae and the people he had not seen for so long. In the intervening time the Ju/'hoansi men had been used as soldiers and guides during the Namibian War of Independence and they and their families had been resettled in Tsumque, a name which means pubic hair – maybe because there was once water from a spring with rushes growing around it. The settlement was made up of a cluster of corrugated-iron shacks, and there was a government trading post run by an angry Afrikaner couple whose job was to distribute food tokens with which the people could buy the cornmeal that had become their staple diet. They also relied on cheap alcohol and cheap tobacco. There was nothing to do here but sit in the dust and get drunk in order to forget.

Marshall's camera moves among the tin shacks. It pauses to watch a drunken fight between two women. Some of the old people recognise him from the old days. They are of course older, but their faces have also been changed by sadness and loss and alcohol and the indignity of their lives. Everyone is dressed in dirty loose-fitting clothes, baseball caps and T-shirts with incongruous slogans printed on them. They mill around in a daze, like the survivors of a war or some other atrocity. They drink and fight and fall over. They lie on the dusty ground and smile lopsided smiles. One woman sings a song:

Death dances with me
We have nothing but the cornmeal they give us
Cornmeal and I hate each other

I sit here and grow old
Death don't come to me
Bitterness is with me now.

I stopped writing in my notebook even though the train was still wheezing and clattering towards its destination. The window of my memory had closed. There was a newspaper on the seat next to me and I read it to find out what was happening on that day as opposed to any other days.

But now that train journey belongs to another time. The world I live in has changed beyond recognition, so that I along with everyone else have been moved to a different place, a place in which death dances with us, as we sit and grow old.

XII

27 April 2020. The chickens have laid three eggs and have trodden on the soft and helpless shell of what is called a wind egg. The cockerel wakes me just before the dawn and it can be that the noise of him tips me back into a deeper sleep, although sometimes I remain awake, surrounded by the vague restlessness that comes from being held as a prisoner within the solitary circumference of my life. This morning I sang 'On the Sunny Side of the Street' before getting up.

> The Bushmen hold fire in their hands when they sing to the stars. They sing to the star that the star may get up high in the sky and that the sun may be warm when it comes out and that the place may not be cold. These are called !khauu ka !kutten !kutten – honey's songs. (//Kabbo)

I have planted sweet peas to cling to the runner beans, although maybe they won't like the idea. I seem to be living a curiously symbolic life in which the behaviour of birds, plants and animals and even the juxtaposition of cups and bowls on the table have taken on a sort of metaphoric power. A robin flew with a soft clunk into a window and died as it lay cradled in the palm of my hand.

It seems as if, in dying, you have taken yourself away from me.

The chronology of my working days has become muddled. Not that it matters; the weeks are rolling into each other with such a casual intimacy and I can hardly distinguish one from the next. I seem to stand at a distance from my own self and from the living and from the dead.

Mother beat the ground and that was when she spoke with the spirit people. She struck a stone and said, 'Oh spirit people, do you no longer think of me? It seems as if you sit with your backs to me. You no longer talk to me as you used to when you still had bodies. You used to talk to me as if you really loved me. But now you seem to have died, leaving your thoughts of me. You seem to have forgotten me. (Dia!kwain)

In order to move on I need to describe Wilhelm Bleek and his sister-in-law Lucy Lloyd and what drove them forward with such dogged determination. The truth is I would prefer to leave them as nothing more than abstract vehicles who made it possible for the words of the /Xam to be recorded and remembered, but I can't do that, so here goes, Bleek first.

Wilhelm Heinrich Immanuel Bleek was born in Berlin in 1827. His father was Professor of Theology at the Berlin University and then in Bonn. As a child Wilhelm was sickly, suffering from eruptions of the skin. As a teenager he read Homer and Le Vaillant's *Travels into the Interior Parts of Africa, by way of the Cape of Good Hope.*

At the age of eighteen he enrolled as an undergraduate at the University of Bonn where he made a study of the original versions of the *Iliad* and the *Odyssey.* He then shifted his interest from Greek and Latin texts to Sanskrit, Arabic, Aramaic and ancient

Egyptian. In trying to imagine him I often allow the image of my dead friend Peter to appear in my mind: big-bodied, awkward men with something of a shared innocence combined with academic brilliance and an almost absurd aptitude for languages. Not that Peter was a linguist by profession; his peculiar genius lay in the mathematics of economics and he was busy with a governmental study of what needed to be done if the pandemic arrived, just a few days before it swept him up and away.

By the age of twenty-three Bleek had become aware of the click languages of the Khoe, the Zulu, the Xhosa and the Sesotho of Southern Africa, and a year later his thesis was the first comprehensive linguistic study of them. He believed there was no such thing as a *savage tongue* and that the dialects of the Khoekhoe herders in particular could be shown to have a close connection with all Indo-European languages. Notwithstanding this, he, along with so many of his contemporaries and perhaps again like my friend Peter, never seemed to question the values of that thing called civilisation and never doubted the European was the most pure incarnation of human being-ness. He saw the European languages, and in his case German, as the evolutionary pinnacle of cultural expression.

Bleek was responsible for creating an extraordinary archive of the /Xam, but it is hard to work out quite how he viewed the people whose language and culture he recorded so meticulously, and there is the sense that, unlike his sister-in-law Lucy Lloyd, he was happy to accept the hierarchy of racial superiority that was so prevalent in his time.

Where else shall we find, unless in the European, that nobly arched head, containing such a quantity of brain? (Charles White, 1799)

Yet, if we wield the sword of extermination as we advance, we have no reason to repine at the havoc committed . . .

Every species which has spread itself from a small point over a wide area, must, in like manner, have marked its progress by the diminution, or the entire extirpation, of some other . . . (Charles Lyell, Darwin's teacher, 1830)

There must be a physical and, consequently, a psychological inferiority in the dark races generally. (Robert Knox, 1850)

They [the savage races] are without a past and without a future. (Frederick Farrar, 1866)

. . . there is no longer room on the globe for Palaeolithic man . . . I do not mean to imply that no efforts were ever made by white men to save them from absolute extinction, or that no Europeans cast an eye of pity upon the unfortunate wanderers . . . Their language with all its clicks and smacking of the lips and guttural sounds . . . was of no use to anyone but themselves and it died with them. They were incompetent to reduce it to writing and too ill-educated to realise the value of the information they possessed. (George McCall Theal, 1911)

XIII

9 May 2020. I woke very early and made a cup of tea and went back to bed with a pencil and an empty blue notebook but I wrote nothing in it.

Now I am in the studio thinking about Wilhelm Bleek. People say that he was a good and kind man, but when I look at the uncertainty that seems to inhabit his face in the photographs, or read what he said about the Bushmen, I am at a loss to know what I think of him. Not that it matters, I simply need to tell the outline of his story in order to fit him into the story of the /Xam.

In 1854 Bleek was on the edge of having a classic nineteenth-century adventure, when he was made Third Officer on an expedition to chart the major rivers of the Congo, the Niger and the Tsadda, in the company of a Dr William Balfour Baikie and a young zoologist called Dalton. They were planning to meet an African explorer called John Beecroft, who had recently been made the governor of the island colony of Fernando Po.

Like characters in a second instalment of *Heart of Darkness*, these three were to travel on a 'schooner fitted with a library and a brass chandelier . . . armed with sabres, pistols, two four-pound cannon . . . a weighty twelve pounder . . . and a supply of quinine to afford assistance' to a missing German explorer. They were also going to bring palm oil and no doubt a good supply of colourful cloth, glass beads and brass wire, along with a few shoddy guns, cheap liquor and tobacco, as a step towards opening up a trade route into the interior.

Stopping in Freetown, Bleek contracted malaria and the fever was still with him when they reached Accra on the Gold Coast. There they were told that Beecroft had just died 'of climate and disease'.

The expedition was cancelled and Bleek returned home. Within a month he received an invitation from the new bishop of Natal, asking him to help compile a Zulu grammar and so in May 1855 off he went to Natal. His first job was to accompany a group of missionaries to Pietermaritzburg in the Drakensberg, acting as their interpreter as they set about converting the heathen. In the Drakensberg mountains Bleek must have seen some of the Bushman rock paintings: wounded elands, running men, a sorcerer with the head of an animal, a striding giant of a woman carrying a spear, all the images so beautiful and intricate that the Europeans were sure they could not have been made by Africans and especially not by Bushmen.

In 1856 he moved to Cape Town to take on the work of cataloguing Governor Grey's library and to act as his official interpreter. By now he had become fascinated by the click languages of the Bushmen, and in 1857 he made his first tentative steps towards understanding /Xam when he arranged to interview three prisoners on Robben Island, but the conditions in prison were very harsh and the prisoners had neither the energy or the freedom to speak to him.

In 1861 Bleek met Jemima Lloyd while she was in Cape Town, on her way back to see her late mother's family in England, who she hadn't seen for twelve years. Just like Lucy, she had quarrelled with her difficult father and was clearly as fiercely independent as her sister. She described her first impressions: 'A German, Dr Bleek by name, has just come to stay here. He is in very bad health. A curious but intelligent face. He is engaged in compiling different native dictionaries and grammars. They say this is a very clever man.'

What started as an intellectual courtship by correspondence quickly led to very tender declarations of love and the two were married in 1862. Sir George Grey had by then left for New Zealand and agreed to leave his book collection to the South African Public Library on condition that Bleek was the curator. And so he and Jemima began their new life in Cape Town and after the first of six children was born they moved to a house called The Hill in the nearby and quiet village of Mowbray.

In 1866 Bleek arranged to meet two Bushman prisoners who had been brought to the Breakwater Jail, and from them, especially from the man known as Adam Kleinhardt (the name in Dutch means small heart), he was able to put together an initial list of words and sentences, written on thin blue paper, cut into strips and stuck into the first of the many notebooks that would become the archive.

Kleinhardt, like most Bushman speakers by this time, had learned basic Afrikaans from working as a farmhand for one of the many Boers who had laid claim to the /Xam homeland. Bleek's Afrikaans was pretty rudimentary, but he had enough to make a bridge of communication. He also used pictures from books and objects that were to be found in the house in order to build up a vocabulary. One of the books was about human anatomy, and from that Bleek was able to find the words for 'her private parts, his private parts, his testicles, my testicles are sore, cap of penis, the rectum, her labia, her vagina, her urethrum, "n gan tan a", "I want to have to do with you" (a man to a woman when he sleeps with her).'

In the late 1860s, Bleek's sister-in-law Lucy Lloyd came to live with the growing family in Mowbray, and as soon as she started helping him with his work, it quickly became apparent that she was a natural linguist.

One of my wife's sisters, of whom two are staying with us, is already further advanced in the practical knowledge of the [/Xam] language than myself, and as she has a far quicker ear I shall have to trust to her observations in many ways. She is of course able to devote more time to this study than I can.

The two of them began to develop a phonetic approximation of the complex sounds they were hearing and learning to enunciate. The sentence *'n gang an yoa'*, 'I shall drink', was spoken, 'as if one clears one's throat, the middle of the tongue at the same time being raised towards the palate and the breath passing out on the left side of the mouth, the right side of the lips being compressed.'

Slowly the nature of a language was beginning to take shape, bringing with it the first intimations of the /Xam as a people and what they had experienced in their recent history.

> Ribs, heart of ox, thy heart, my heart is sore, ox lungs, ox lung, my lungs are sore, ox liver, my liver is sore. The Bushmen eat the cattle of the Boers, the Boers take the children of the Bushmen. Calf, one calf, two calves, many calves. (Adam Kleinhardt)

> The Dutchman is wicked, the Bushman is small. The Dutchman has cattle. The Bushmen have no cattle. The Bushman take the cattle of the Dutchmen. The Dutchmen seek their cattle. (Adam Kleinhardt)

XIV

11 May 2020. There was a full moon three days ago; so bright it seemed to have punctured a hole in the darkness. I sat for a while on one of the four pretty metal chairs that are gathered convivially around a table in the garden and remembered painting them red a long time ago. I stared at the pale shimmering face of the moon looking down on me until I grew cold, or maybe I grew sad, I am no longer sure.

> The moon comes out of the mountain. He climbs into the sky. He runs into the clouds. The stars follow the moon. They come out of the clouds and walk in the sky. They are many. The mother star leads the child star by the hand. She is great. She is upright. She is red. (//Kabbo)

Two days ago was the anniversary for the end of the last world war, with bunting strung like Christmas lights from many of the houses in this little village and Union Jacks flapping from the walls. I passed a portrait of the Queen, smiling, when she was young, and one of Winston Churchill whose fat ghost has inexplicably returned to this country, as if he might be able to answer questions no one else knows how to answer.

It was a beautiful day and I went for a walk along a different stretch of the North Sea and it was quieter and more benevolent than when I last saw it. The path through the reeds was alive with the chittering of little birds.

When I got home I climbed the steps to my husband's studio, thinking of doing some writing. The door was partly open and a kestrel had entered and was flapping and crashing against a closed window. I opened the door as wide as it would go, but the bird continued battering at the glass, every so often pausing to stare out, furious with the closeness of a sky it could not reach. In the brief moments when it was still, I admired the black delineations around the eyes like the prow of an Egyptian ship, the apricot tinge of the facial feathers, the streamlined energy of the body.

A pond-dipping net was leaning against a wall in the studio, and because I was afraid the kestrel would soon knock itself unconscious, I gave it a gentle swoop with the net towards the open door that leads into the garden. It didn't seem to mind being persuaded to move like that, but settled just above the door and was briefly still as it confronted the barrier of another pane of glass. The glare of the sunlight delineated the silhouette of its profile and the sharp curve of the beak, but then it returned to the angry battering. Once more I swooped with the net and this time the kestrel flew into the garden and it was as if it had never been.

The following day it was suddenly cold with a wind whipping in all directions at once. That evening I again did my best to protect the young plants in the vegetable patch, urgently wanting to keep them alive because they seemed to hold the promise of a future taking shape. I think of my family: three groups of them scattered in places I cannot reach. I see their faces on a computer screen and long for the scent of hair, the touch of a hand, the fact of breathing.

So here I am with young broad beans and chard, young sweet peas and tomatoes. The guinea pigs are definitely becoming less fearful, but they are all males and have started to fight each other so fiercely they sometimes draw blood, so I need to do something. The cockerel announces the dawn while the night is still pitch-black.

Bleek's house in Mowbray looks nice in the photographs I have seen, a friendly building and a big garden set against the backdrop of the mountain known as Devil's Peak. Arum lilies and snapdragons filled the flower beds, and there were vegetable beds and chickens, as well as a cow, a horse and a donkey called Neddie. The livestock were kept in outhouses at the far end of the garden, while a cat, a dog and a parrot lived in the house. This was long before the thought of the need for the guard dogs I saw or heard in Cape Town and in the Karoo; their threatening and hysterical presence held within elegant gardens or in the compounds around a farm. Everywhere I went in the city and in the countryside I was also confronted by the image of the black silhouette of a dog with its teeth bared, reproduced on metal signs fixed to the electrified fences that define ownership and keep out intruders.

Bleek made a rough drawing of the ground-floor plan of his house, showing a kitchen, a study, a dining room and a sitting room. There must have been an extra room or two at the back where the /Xam who came to stay over the years that followed were accommodated, or it might be that they were lodged in one of the outhouses, no one seems to be quite sure. Certainly they were interviewed in the garden when the weather was mild, or in Bleek's study when it was not, or in the sitting room when it was Lucy recording their words in one of many notebooks.

The project began after Bleek heard that twenty-eight Bushmen were being held in the Breakwater Jail. He wrote to the new governor saying he would like to visit them to make a study of their language, 'because its apparently primitive character promises to throw great light upon many important questions on the origin and development of speech.' Permission was granted, and between 1869 and 1870 he and Lucy conducted the initial interviews of possible informants.

It was agreed that a prisoner could be transferred to the house in Mowbray in order to pursue the work in a more convivial setting. The prison chaplain made the choice of a young man called /A!kunta, whose name means 'cannot come in!' He was called Klaas Stoffel by the Boer farmer for whom he had worked. For the first five months a guard was installed with him, to make sure he did not escape, but then the guard left and he stayed at The Hill long after his sentence had expired.

According to the Breakwater Jail records /A!kunta was a Hottentot which was the odd and derogatory European name for the cattle-herding Khoekhoe people who were related to the /Xam but followed a very different way of life. He was just under five feet tall, had a mole on his left temple, small moles on his right cheek, brown marks on his left arm and *no religion*. He was described as being 'intelligent' and 'the best behaved Bushman boy', whatever that might mean. From the two photographs that were taken of him later in a studio he looks terribly young, although he was married to a woman called /Ka! whose whereabouts he did not know. In one photograph you see his head and bare chest, one nipple incongruously revealed, and in the other he is in profile, wearing a thick checked shirt. He appears to be a serious and gentle person, but again there is that expression of abstracted despair in his face. Under the second photograph Lucy Lloyd wrote, 'A. 1st Bushman, got at Breakwater.'

/A!kunta was still a teenager when he was captured and brought to Cape Town in 1869. He had seen a lot of bloodshed and had experienced starvation which was compounded by his treatment as a prisoner. He was so thin and weak it was thought that he was suffering from consumption and might soon be dead.

He was born around 1852, in an area that holds the cluster of low hills known as the Strandberg, although the original name was said to be Strontberg, or shit mountain, maybe because the black boulders scattered across them looked like balls of *stront* or shit or because of the battles there which caused a lot of death among the /Xam, but also among the Boers who were killed by the poison-tipped arrows. When I was in the Karoo we were planning to drive along a dirt track to the foot of that hill in order to walk up to see the engraved boulders, but the farmer had forgotten to unlock the gate for us. '/A!kunta: cannot come in!' I thought as we drove on.

Because of the locked gate I never saw the rock drawings that /A!kunta had known, nor could I look down at the flat plains surrounding the hills of his childhood. On that day in March, the land was dry and barren, but apparently when the rains come everything is transformed as if by magic into lush grasslands. In previous times the rain also heralded the arrival of the springbok, jumping and twisting in the air with something like a mixture of fear and delight.

> The water shall rain, bringing the young springbok . . .
> another winter shall come . . . the people are shooting the
> 'warm spring's' springbok. The people are hunting the
> warm sun's ostriches. (//Kabbo)

The springbok, along with the kudu and the eland, the ostrich, quagga and lion and the great herds of elephants are all remembered on the rocks, but most of the animals of /A!kunta's childhood had either vanished or they were fast disappearing. He thought elephants were mythological creatures that heralded the rain. An old Bushman had told him about a creature called the kudu but he had never seen one.

In 1857 the Cape government made a new law that extended the land rights of the settlers as far as the Orange River. /A!kunta called this the Big River and it encompassed all the territory around the Strandberg. In 1859 there were still many /Xam in the region, but by 1863 only around five hundred of them were thought to have survived and they were starving and destitute.

> Give bread. Give bread that I may eat. Give meat that I
> may . . . (Note by Lucy Lloyd written on a scrap of paper
> on the inside cover of notebook)

Along with //Kabbo, /A!kunta had been part of the so-called Tooren Gang which was 'mopped up' by British troops. He was accused of eating part of an ox and sentenced to two years of hard labour. He was with //Kabbo on that same slow journey to Cape Town.

When /A!kunta was brought to live at The Hill in 1870, he was given work to do in the garden and he saved the money he earned to buy a violin, which according to one of Bleek's daughters he learned to play 'with a talent that would have graced a far better instrument', but much of every day was spent in helping to build up a /Xam vocabulary and then answering questions. At first Bleek was very much the leader of the enterprise. His handwriting in the notebooks is large and to me, at least, it looks impatient. He wanted to collect what he called Bushman fables, but was not particularly interested in the men who knew the fables or in what they might think about the world in which they found themselves.

Lloyd's handwriting is more careful, precise and somehow self-effacing. She considered herself as nothing more than the great man's assistant and he appears to have been happy to see her in that light, referring in a publication that came out just after his death in 1875 to 'the valuable assistance which I have derived from the collections made for me by L . . .' even though she had done the majority of the interviews herself. In the codicil to his will he 'gratefully acknowledged the great help she has been to me in my literary labours' while requesting her from beyond the grave 'to work well out our joint Bushman studies'. And this she did, against all the odds, right up to her own death in 1914.

Lucy was clearly a very receptive listener, increasingly aware of the underlying story of loss and displacement that she was hearing, while respecting the personalities of the people who were talking to her. She observed all of her informants with a writer's eye and often made little notes about things they remarked on that had nothing to do with the main body of a narrative. The interviews were clearly very relaxed as the conversations moved from one topic to another, from a dream to a practical observation then to a sudden step into the huge landscape of the mythic past of the /Xam.

One of Lucy's first notebooks is a little soft-backed pamphlet, and although she kept it, she later added a short apology on the opening page:

> Got at Breakwater and much of it I can even now see is very wrong, but I keep it partly for use and partly for the curiosity of the 1st attempt at hearing this difficult language.

Inside the front cover she had left a folded piece of paper on which she wrote '1st Bushman (L.) got at Breakwater' and this was followed by a simple vocabulary:

gun
small
the pipe is here
cough
he coughs
walk
crawl
roll
sit
sleep
hold
beat
scratch
shake
water
horse
neck
butterfly

Slowly a recording system began to take shape, and once a certain number of /Xam words with the same opening sound had been gathered, they were cut out in strips and stuck into a notebook. During the one short day I spent looking at the archive in the Cape Town University Library, I copied a few entries from one of the early vocabularies that Lucy made with /A!kunta and I was startled by how much meaning and metaphor the words were somehow able to hold.

thu: white man
thu thu: baboon
tna!karita: shadow
turruwa: to forget (the past)
tzarra: another, different
!koa: bones
!ko: to dance
!koa kken: full moon (the moon was said to be full with the bodies of the dead)

As he gathered confidence, /A!kunta began to comment on the work that was being done. He was particularly fascinated by the ink drying on the paper and the shadow on the page as the writing hand passed over it.

I imagine them sitting side by side in the pretty English garden, speaking against the backdrop of the lowing of the cow, the barking of the dog, the heehawing of the donkey, or in the sitting room where there was a sewing machine, needles, buttons and other domestic items, religious or pastoral paintings on the wall no doubt, and a few books in a bookcase. Perhaps sometimes they worked in Bleek's study where the more erudite leather-bound books were kept, the inkwell and the black paperweight on the heavy table, the ticking clock on the mantelpiece, and little displays of Bushman artefacts that were part of the hunter-gatherer way of life:

a brush called /ku, made of the hair of the animal called /gipp. The handle is made from the stem of the thorn bush called !nabba. It is bound with springbok neck sinew, wai!kauka /kurri. The women stir the soup with the pointed end of the handle and also lift the meat from the pot with it. They use the brush to eat soup, dipping it in and carrying it to their mouth. They use a !lau, a gemsbok rib for peeling and eating /kui. It is marked with little holes, bored in on the inside in seven rows as its owner's mark . . .

I see /A!kunta perched on a chair that is too big for him, explaining the nature and the names of the things that belong to his world to the unassuming little Englishwoman who is always accompanied by the noisy rustle of her crinoline dresses. Wherever they are working, the notebooks, pens and pencils are with them.

Bit by bit /A!kunta's fragmented story began to take shape. His father was !Haken-/ya and his mother was Ttoa-ken-an. Of one grandfather he said, 'The lion killed him at night. The lion comes. The lion grasps him at night.' A grandmother was also killed by a lion. By the time he was fifteen, all the land of his people was in the hands of Boers and he was working for a farmer called Piet Swart and 'living in a Bush-house with springbok skins over it.' Once he felt a bit safer he told Lucy he had been very afraid of his master and of all the Boers, 'but now I am not scared any more.'

As he is knocking me down with a stick, he thinks I shall be dead. My heart is not sweet, my heart goes around quick. I must quickly go so that the water can cool my wounds. The water washes off the blood. (/A!kunta)

Three months after his arrival at the Bleek household, /A!kunta was telling of the old woman who was eaten by the hyena's mother. When I was in the Karoo I visited an area that I would never be able to find again however hard I looked: an almost featureless terrain on which a few round stones in a loose circle denoted the outer circumference of dwelling places which still held the grinding stones the people had used, as well as flint tools and arrowheads and pieces of ostrich shell cut into round and tiny beads, so perfect they seemed to have been made with the precision of a modern machine, and sometimes, among the stones and the sand, the dark stain of charcoal from a fire.

This is /A!kunta's story of one such settlement: the hunger among his people, the fragility of life and the closeness of death.

The old woman lies in an old deserted house, her sons having left her having previously closed the circle (the sides) of the house, including the door opening, with the sticks from other people's houses, for the old woman cannot walk out. They left her a nice fire in the house with some more dried wood which they fetched for her and they left the top of the house open so that she could feel the warmth of the sun. They left her because they were all starving and they went to seek food at some other place, she not being strong enough to go with them. The old hyena, the hyena's mother, takes, takes up the old woman, while the old woman lies in the old house.

XV

30 May 2020. The continuity of sunshine has not been broken, but two weeks have gone by during which I abandoned my fragile book in order to teach some university students on Zoom. I briefly met twenty-four strangers and spoke to them one by one about their work and what they wanted from it. There were also three talks to a gathering of faces the size of large-letter postage stamps, with questions afterwards: a yellow rectangle shining around the person who wished to say something. What is the difference between fiction and non-fiction? How do you go about research? Do you always tell the truth? Have you ever hurt people with what you have said?

Returning to the studio where I had been writing, I was shocked by the chaos I found there. It looked as if I had been called out to a sudden emergency: typewritten pages and pencilled notes scattered all over the floor and spilling off the table, files lying open, books lying face down, a half-eaten apple turned brown and soggy, a cold cup of coffee with a milky scum shining on its surface.

But now I am here again and a bit of order has been restored and I am more or less ready to begin. Through the open door I can see the vegetable bed; the broad beans staring towards me in the dappled sunlight and the bright orange splashes of colour from the first nasturtium flowers. A soft wind is moving the branches of the young quince tree that has its roots planted in a handful of my husband's ashes.

Whatever I do or do not do, part of me is caught in the confusion that surrounds us all on all sides. Our leader is mostly silent and when he does speak he appears wide-eyed with something like fear and almost incoherent. Somewhere close by there is his friend and adviser, a man whose angular limbs, jerky movements and strange rubbery face make him seem like a cartoon character from a rather scary film; I sometimes expect his eyes to pop out on stalks, his lips to slip down beneath his chin.

'We are closed in and the key is turned on our uncertainty.' My father taught me that line from Yeats when I was very young but I have never much thought of it until now.

Once again I need to move on, or back, or sideways, into some parallel world where I can walk more freely than I can here and so I am looking more closely at the Englishwoman called Lucy Lloyd. It's 1870 and she is thirty-six years old and from the photographs she appears small and slight-bodied, with a mixture of intelligence, timidity and defiance in her gaze. Her pale, straight hair is severely parted and pulled into a bun at the nape of her neck. According to the fashion of the day she wears a tight bodice and a voluminous skirt made solid by the wire hoops that hold it. Again I think of the rustle of her walking and how strange it must have been to see women dressed like this, floating heads with no skin of the body visible apart from the fluttering white hands.

Lucy was fond of her mother, but her mother died when she was young. By all accounts, her father was an unpleasant bully and when he remarried her stepmother proved to be a confused and angry woman, overwhelmed by the birth of her twelve children.

Lucy suffered all her life from illness as well as sadness, and I imagine this could be seen in her movements as well as in her manner. She had never considered herself to be beautiful, and although she was once about to marry, the engagement was called off as a result of some malicious gossip, and then the man himself died tragically, while the woman who was to have been his wife remained single and filled with remorse.

But once she had moved into the Bleek household and had started to work on his /Xam project, Lucy was able to discover the companionship of her own mind and its workings and that seems to have satisfied her and made her much more content. The people of Cape Town found the entire household and their Bushmen guests both odd and shocking, but it is clear that Lucy was able to relax in the satisfaction of her work and in the company of her three sisters, her young nieces and her brother-in-law Wilhelm.

Reading some of the notes she made while writing down the words spoken to her by /A!kunta, //Kabbo, /Han‡kass'o and Dia!kwain, and all the others, there is a sense that with them and with the world they allowed her to enter, she found a way of being herself and she never let that go for the rest of her life. It makes sense.

Towards the end of 1870, Lucy, along with Bleek and /A!kunta, went back to the Breakwater Jail in search of a second informant. The old man called //Kabbo was chosen and in February 1871 he came to live at The Hill and a new conversation began.

My master had taken Stoffel [/A!kunta]. While Stoffel was working there, my master went and told me I should come to him. He said so. I agreed that I would do so. I came to be with Stoffel.

On 30 May 1871 Lucy and //Kabbo visited the South African Museum of Natural History. It must have been quite startling to see a white woman accompanied by a Bushman who was clearly not her servant; the two of them walking side by side through the Company's Gardens and up the white marble steps that led into a building filled with images of British royals and colonial dignitaries, alongside ornate plasterwork, mirrors and sweeping staircases with mahogany banisters.

When I was there in a time that already feels so long ago, so far away, it was a hot day and I remember a larger-than-life statue of Sir Cecil Rhodes, standing in the sunshine, his left arm raised in a rather dangerous salute, his hand pointing towards the unconquered lands to the north. My first impression on entering the museum building was of its bright whiteness, but above all else it was the shock at seeing the size and number of the glass cabinets, room after room of them built to hold representatives of all the life of this country from a straight-necked giraffe down to a locust and a tiny shrew mouse.

But here they are in 1871, the white woman in a rustling dress and the Bushman called //Kabbo, walking together through the South African Museum of Natural History. I imagine him wearing the same red flannel shirt, heavy brown jacket and thick trousers that he wears in a portrait made of him in this same year. In the portrait he has an earring in one ear, threaded with a single red bead that echoes the red of his shirt.

Lucy and //Kabbo pause in front of the crowded glass cases, and in a strange variation of Adam's task in Paradise, he names the familiar creatures that parade before his eyes.

> The cat, the wild cat, is here, he sits looking. The leopard he sits. The wild dog he stands. The giraffe he stands. The baboon it eats honey. The ichneumon sits on a tree. It nods its head when it sees rain clouds.

The lion in the glass case has its mouth open in a perpetual roar. Does //Kabbo find it frightening or sad to see it here? His name means Dream and maybe these silent animals that do not attack or run away when he approaches them seem to emerge from out of a dream.

He moves steadily on: pangolin and aardvark, spotted hyena and Cape hunting dog, civet and slender mongoose, honey badger and quagga, sable antelope, kudu and eland. He knows them all as part of who he is and each one in turn comes alive as he speaks its /Xam name.

When a man kills something he is cold, his wind is cold. When he kills anything, he is cold, for the thing's wind is not a little cold. The people say, 'Our brother there, his wind feels like this when he makes a kill. His wind is so cold.' (Dia!kwain)

The people eat ostriches, they eat gambro cucumbers, they eat ant eggs, they eat honey, they eat edible bulbs, they drink the yolk of ostrich eggs with a brush made from the tail of the gemsbok antelope. The people eat jackal, they eat great hares, they eat springbok. They make shoes of kudu skin, they make shoes of eland skin, they eat anteater meat, they shoe themselves with anteater skin shoes. (Dia!kwain)

XVI

7 June 2020. Rain. A small cold wind. The chickens bedraggled. The tomato plants also. I would say there is no celebration of birdsong, but I just heard a robin briefly rippling the air and then a blackbird.

Two days ago I went to visit my friend Jayne whose husband died of corona in April. We now call it Covid, a word that makes me think of the crow family: the rooks that scatter in such numbers across the meadow beyond this garden, and the one for sorrow two for joy magpies which must have a nest close by, because one or the other comes every day to do awkward battle with the peanuts in their wire container.

The two-hour journey to the north Norfolk coast felt like a huge and daring adventure. I passed through places I know well, but a blanket of quietness had changed them almost beyond recognition and I drove straight through the empty centre of the city of Norwich, with only traffic lights to slow me down. When we met, Jayne and I performed that strange one step forward two steps back dance we all use these days, accompanied by the uncertain laughter that goes with it. Dipping down, as the old Bushman said, 'in those days we could not be together. We had to scatter. We had to dip down, dip down, and scatter.'

We went to the sea. A short walk across the absurd neatness

of a golf course where men and women in little vehicles moved over the close-clipped grass like figures in a board game. And then there it was, wide and grey and stretching out towards the Arctic. The tide was high and so we walked across the massed banks of pebbles, the huge beetling cliffs of sand towering above us as tall as skyscrapers and very unstable, and I saw fresh heaps of their collapse as I passed beneath them, but not too close. We had a picnic sitting on the remains of a sea defence which is now nothing more than a little cluster of storm-bleached wooden posts emerging from the pebbles and bolted together with rusting bolts. I was discombobulated by the bright flashes of sunshine: a nocturnal animal brought out of its burrow and blinking in the light.

9 June 2020. When I got back my thoughts began to race, especially at night: a rattling wheel of questions without any answers, doubts without access to any reassurance. I only slept for maybe two or three hours for one night, two nights, three nights, four nights and from being very tired I became convinced I was ill, even though the only symptom was a heavy head and a dry mouth that accompanied it as a sort of paying guest.

I started crying when I remembered standing on the round body of a mountain in northern Italy that I know well, and from there you can look out across an undulating ocean of other mountains and the Alpine swifts scream as they race through the high air and once one of them brushed against my cheek, and it was that recollection of physical contact which made the tears flow. And then I cried again as I thought I knew I was dying and I imagined saying goodbye to my children and my children's children, and in the moment of parting I realised that nothing mattered in all the world beyond the tribe of family, the genetic nest. I told them this in my thoughts and they stared at me with serious eyes.

'We are few. It was so.'

I spoke to a friend and he brought me three little pills with a strange name, and thanks to them I slept for ten hours for three nights in a row and each morning I woke feeling empty and odd but less absent, less on edge. I used up some of the blank hours of those days by going through the PDF of the Bleek archive, printing out the pages I thought I might want to refer to later. It was a very automatic process, but it kept me quiet and gave me the sense of having something to show as evidence of the passing of time. It is odd, how I have pinned myself to the written word, pinned my own survival to the completion of the story I am telling.

The weather is cold and damp and grey, but the battering of the wind of yesterday has ceased, and now in order to return to where I was, or close to where I was, I thought to include a story about a man who dies after wounding himself accidentally on his own poisoned arrow.

It is April 1872 and //Kabbo is talking to Lucy. His conversation makes huge and sudden leaps in all sorts of directions, while the central story he is telling evolves over numerous pages with many diversions and repetitions. It is a form of narration called *kumm!* and //Kabbo is very good at it. At one point he is speaking in the voice of a lion that has killed a gemsbok.

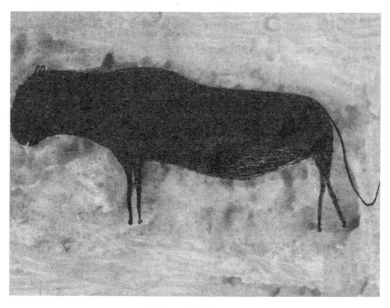

Dia!kwain's lioness

I must eat the gemsbok for I am hungry. I must lay the gemsbok against the //kerri thorn tree. I shall sleep, leaning against the gemsbok in the dark. The jackals come, they smell my smell. They shall fear me . . . They walking, turn back while I lying look (at them) . . . I shall afterwards eat again, while I feel that my stomach hungers . . . my body shall become cool as I lie under the //kerri's shade, for midday is here.

He continues:

My thoughts spoke to me, therefore my mouth speaks to you. I thought in the night while I lay, I thought that you should give me thread. I should sew, sewing the buttons afterwards on the jacket. The buttons which you gave me, for otherwise they would be falling down upon the ground.

He speaks of death:

The Bushman dies, he goes to this place; the old man becomes lean, he starves, he dies, he goes to this place. The old woman becomes lean, her flesh vanishes away, she dies, she goes to this place. The little child who is very small, it dies, it goes to this place.

And then he begins a long account of the hunter who dies and how his wife and his people deal with the tragedy. The story covers some twenty pages in the notebook and this is a part of it.

A man leaves the house to hunt springbok. He gently runs. He falls. He pierces himself with his own arrow. The wound mouth is not good.

The people who were with him came close to the spring-bok, but now they do not carry the body of the springbok, they carry the body of the man.

The wounded man is brought to his wife. He says to her, 'I feel that I shall die, for the wound is large, the pain of the wound is great.'

He says to her, 'fetch fire's wood and make a fire for me. I shall not see another day break, for I shall die in the night, my heart will fall. The people will cry in the morning.

'The boys and girls must bring water for you. The boys must follow the vulture scent to find springbok for you. They must seek tortoises and bring them to you. They must act well, for they are grown and I die, leaving them. I do not come back to live again.'

The wounded man says, ' I shall think of you, my wife, when I am dead. I will see if you get food. I will see if you are warm. I will think of our children. Your brothers must look after you. They must give you fat to rub on your body so your body is beautiful.

'You must place me on my cloak of skin covered with blood. That is where I must lie. You will watch over me. You will cry for me. You will sit and look at me.

'The time of talk is over. I am still. I shall not speak in the darkness. I am holding your heart.'

The man's wife says, 'My heart thinks my husband was not a little handsome. My heart thinks he was not a little good. He dies as a young man and my heart thinks of him and is shocked. He ran fast hunting springbok and now my heart trembles and is startled because he said to me his death is near.

'We were young when we married, he had not yet grown a beard on his face. Now I cry because he dies from

99

me. I do not want to eat because of my thoughts. The people must lift him up, the man who lies here, they must carry him and put him in the hole. They must cover him with earth.

'I go to my father who lives close to the water, that I may drink and my children may drink. I shall cry by the water while I live with my father who lives close to the water. I grew up there. I drank the water there.

'The children's bodies are pale. I see their father in them for their faces resemble their father, their eyebrows resemble their father's eyebrows, their eyes resemble their father's eyes. Therefore while I sat looking at the little boys as they returned to me, it was as if I saw their father as he walking came.'

XVII

11 June 2020 and I still have the feeling of being locked down, even though the lock has lifted a bit and I can enter a bubble, which sounds like a very fragile and unreliable thing to enter. I never dreamt I would prove so acquiescent to so many new and changing rules of behaviour.

My son says he will soon drive up from Bristol, leaving his wife and two young children at home. Two days. I think we can hug, or maybe we cannot hug. We can sit inside the house and talk. We can walk by the sea with the wind blowing and talk. We can eat together and drink some wine and talk about other things and not talk about politics and the virus.

> In the past the wind's son was a person. He became a bird
> and he flies. He does not walk as he used to, for he flies.
> He lives in the mountain. (//Kabbo)

I'll be seventy-two in a couple of months. Hair as pale as my mother's hair once was. Nothing physically wrong with me as far as I can tell, but the story of my life is there in my face, and I have a loose softness of body that surprises me. Sometimes my limbs ache in the morning as if they need to recover from a long journey, which I suppose they do. My children are tender and kind, and if I were to be ill, I know that one or other of them would do their best to take care of me. The fact of love is there and undeniable but in these lockdown times I keep thinking of the story of the old woman who was left behind in a dwelling place, because she had not the strength to travel. Her family has no choice. They must go and search for food or else they would all die.

I imagine what it was like to be her. I allow myself to think her thoughts as she sits within the confinement of a hut and death moves inexorably closer. She knows that she is loved, but in the circumstances, love cannot help her. I try to step over the separation of time and place, in order to become this other old woman and to speak her thoughts:

I cannot walk with them and so they must leave me here. They gave me wood for a fire. They gave me an ostrich eggshell that holds the roasted and ground-up bodies of a few locusts and I can put the dust to my tongue and call it food. They gave me another ostrich eggshell filled with water that has a bitter taste to it, so that I can drink at the house of water. The hole in the shell is sealed with mud, not with beeswax because the bees have gone from where they were, along with the springbok, the tortoise, the hare. Famine is here. The ostrich eggs are strong. They are decorated with black lines that tell stories I already know, or new stories that will come to me as I look at the lines.

My people gave me a few gambro roots to chew and a handful of little pieces of the plant called driedoorn by the Boers. The driedoorn leaves a sweet spicy taste in your mouth, as if you have eaten something nice and this is the memory of it.

My people made the dwelling place more secure with branches and grass taken from th other dwelling places which are empty. They closed the door of my dwelling place with branches so that I am safe.

They lit the fire for me and there is a hole in the roof above it

102

through which the smoke can escape. I must keep the fire alive during the night so that the small flames and the smell of wood smoke and wood ash will frighten the animals who move in the dark. 'The grown man is the one who listens and knows if a beast of prey is walking about, smelling the hut's scent, that it may kill a person there'.

On the first night there was no moon, but I saw the Milky Way. 'My mother was the one who told me that the girl arose; she put her hands into the wood ashes; she threw up the wood ashes into the sky. She said to the wood ashes, 'The wood ashes which are here, they must altogether become the Milky Way . . . The Milky Way gently glows; while it feels that it is wood ashes . . . while it feels that the girl was the one who said that the Milky Way should give a little light for the people, that they might return home by night. (/Han‡kass'o)

The night was long because I was alone. The dawn did not quickly break. Coldness sat upon the earth and the coldness was such that it felt as if the fire had disappeared . . . The sun crossed over. It went into the sky when it was hot and I ate some of the gambro roots. I chewed the leaves of the driedoorn bush. I tasted the locust powder. I drank bitter water from the ostrich shell.

Another night and I watched the stars in the sky through the hole in the roof. 'Our mothers told me a star resembles our heart. The stars are used to know the time at which we die. When we were alive it seems our hearts stood upright. At the time in which we die, our heart falls down. Therefore the stars dying away noise takes our hearts with it. The star tells other people who did not know, that we have died.' (/Han‡kass'o) 'The people dying go away. Things that are flesh must dying go away, for they feel that they walk on the earth. The moon feels that it sails in the sky. It walks in the dark. It sails in the darkness.' (/A!kunta)

I am the old woman in the old hut. I wait for the old hyena who is coming soon to take me. As I wait I sing:

The old pot must remain
For I lie in the old hut.
The old soup brush must remain
For I lie in the old hut.
The old kaross must remain
For I lie in the old hut.
The old bed must remain
For I lie in the old hut.
The old dish must remain
For I lie in the old hut. (/Han‡kass'o)

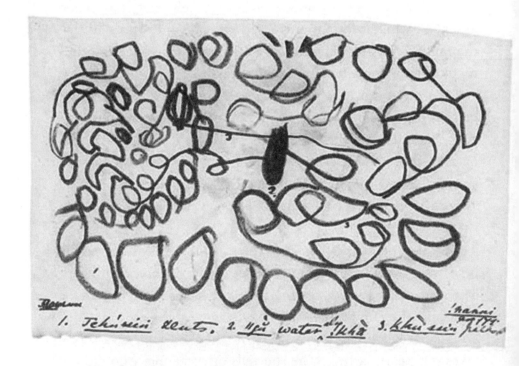

Dwelling places. (!Nanni)

XVIII

28 June 2020. My son arrives. We hold hands and stare at each other, familiar eyes to familiar eyes, and then we wash our hands with the shame of the fear of our own skin.

> It seemed as if the wind cried with her, when her tears fell. Then the wind did not want her eye's tears to fall. (Dia!kwain)

We drive to the sea and walk beside it. Much more of the fragile cliff edge has tumbled down since I was last here. Tufts of green grass hold on to chunks of pale soil that lie scattered on the pebbles of the shore. The sand martins have lost many of their nesting sites, but those that remain are chattering and swooping in the air above our heads.

> The things that are in the sky, we see in the water, when we stand at the water's edge. We see all things when we stand at the water's edge. We see the stars that look like fires which burn. When it is night another man walks. It seems as if it were midday when he walks by the water. We see him clearly, even though he is distant. (Dia!kwain)

Both of us look for fossils as we walk, because this is what we always do here; it is a good place to find them. He picks up a brown lump of bone, no bigger than a plum and as heavy as the stone it has turned into. I find a smaller thing which has the telltale swirl of energy that shows it was once part of a living creature. I do not know what beast it came from, but I can see that it is a single vertebra, from a neck perhaps. Three years ago my son broke a vertebra in his neck when he was diving in a pool that was supposed to be safe, but it held a concrete block lying in wait for him like Beowulf's water monster. He could have died from the impact and when I went to see him that night lying in a hospital bed there was the distant stare of death in his eyes. But he did not die. I give him the vertebra. He puts it in his pocket.

We go swimming. The water is murky but friendly. It is my first swim this year. I am content, safe within the bubble of time and place that surrounds me.

My son leaves and I hold the memory of his having been here. Both my children say they will come towards the end of July with their families; even my daughter-in-law's parents will come. I have never been so aware of being part of a tribe, holding together as an aspect of survival. It makes me think of //Kabbo when he and those who were with him were caught in a 'mopping up operation'.

There is my wife, there am I, there is my son's wife, there is my daughter, she carries a child who is very small, there is my daughter's husband. We are few. It was so.

With the passing of the months //Kabbo's language is becoming easier for Lucy to understand and there is less and less need for them to supplement what they say with simple Afrikaans. He calls her Mistress while calling Wilhelm Bleek Magistrate, which seems like a rather ominous title that bestows the power to give life or death, imprisonment or freedom.

//Kabbo sits in the garden, the study, the sitting room. He talks to these big white strangers, answering their questions, telling them what he knows. Bleek wants to know how the stars and the moon were made, how death came, what /Kaggen the Mantis said. Lucy does not seem to mind what //Kabbo speaks of. She listens to whatever he says and writes everything down.

> //Kabbo was the second child of !Kui ang. !Kui ang's father was Ttono wo. The rhinoceros killed Ttono wo with its horns. It threw him up to the sky. He fell to the ground. He died because the rhinoceros had thrown him up to the sky. (/A!kunta)

Over the period of more than two years that //Kabbo stays here in this house, the three of them learn to understand each other, but it is to Lucy that he speaks of his thoughts and his memories and what his dreams show him. One morning he tells her he dreamt of a lion which spoke and the lion was with other lions.

> I saw them. They were black. Their feet resembled the lion. I feared them. Their legs were many. They had hair. Their tails were long. I was afraid. I was startled awake . . . Going, they said they would find springbok by following their spoor . . . I saw the springbok spoor, and the tracks the lions had left. I was startled awake. (//Kabbo)

On another night he dreamt he was talking with his wife !Kwabba-ang. She is far away, near his old place of the bitter water and near to !Kau-/nunu, which the Boers call Kenhardt. In the dream his wife asks him for tobacco and in the dream he gives her a pipe to smoke. She wants to know whose pipe it is. He says it belongs to him. He says he is staying at the house of people who are different.

> She did say that I did not return to her. She asked if I did still work; that I had not returned to her. I said to her that I did not work; for I have been teaching here. She said to me she had seen springbok. She did not eat springbok. I told her I had been waiting to get her. /Han‡kass'o was to have brought her to me. I said so. I talked to her. I was startled awake.

//Kabbo's prison term is over but he continues to stay with the Mistress and the Magistrate in the house called The Hill in the village called Mowbray. Perhaps he is afraid to return to his home, only to find it is no longer his home and no longer a place he can recognise. Or it could be that he stays because in having his words understood and written down in books, he feels he can keep his people alive, both the living and the dead; all of them scattered but held together by the power of his stories, the power of his memories. He is explaining who they are and who they once were; the time of their being stretching back and back to the moment when one of the First at Sitting People pushed the sun up into the sky and the sun raised an arm and released the light of the dawn on the earth.

//Kabbo speaks on behalf of all of his people: a stream of thoughts and associations in which one subject rolls into the next. While telling his stories he notices the inkwell, the clock, the book, the lowing of the cow he had to tend to in the early morning when he woke from his dream. He moves with ease from talking about the button that has come off his jacket, to speaking in the voice of a lion.

He has feet with which he is a lion. He has hands with which he is a man. He talks. He eats people when he is a man, because he feels he is a lion's man. He catches people at night because he shines with his eyes which are like fire.

Several of those who have written about //Kabbo and have studied his words say that the longer he stays in Mowbray, the more romantic his memory of his old life becomes, but perhaps it's not quite like that. He is far from everywhere that is familiar and yet in his mind he is able to enter and inhabit the places he once knew as his own and the life that those places held. For him, as for all of his people, there is nothing to separate the past from the present, the living from the dead, the lion who speaks from the man who speaks. //Kabbo is able to go home without leaving the village of Mowbray. He follows the path. The trees are tall. The path is long. The water is bitter. The springbok are numerous.

It is now almost two years since his son-in-law /Han‡kass'o set off north in the direction of Bitterpits to try to find !Kwabba-ang and their daughter and bring them back to Mowbray, but he still has not returned. When he left /Han‡kass'o wore a new pair of trousers given to him by Bleek and he carried a letter written in English, intended as protection if a white man wanted to know what this Bushman was doing, where he was going and was he dangerous and should he therefore be killed just in case. Since then there has been no word, no sign.

In July 1873, the coldest month of the year //Kabbo made it clear that he would stay until the spring and then he had to leave no matter what. Apparently he had often asked Bleek if he would ask *the Groot Baas* – the Big Boss, Sir Henry Barkly – to '*drive away*' *the farmers from the water and the hunting grounds which belonged to the Bushmen*. He also wanted to be reassured that Bleek would keep the promise he had made and give him a new pair of boots to walk the long journey back home and a rifle so he could hunt for game.

I must possess a gun, feeding myself so I do not eat my fellow's food. A gun takes care of an old man, it is the one that shoots the springbok which we eat in the cold wind. With our bodies filled we lie down in our houses in the cold wind. The gun is the one which is strong. It satisfies a man's hunger, in the middle of the cold.

In his mind //Kabbo has already arrived at the place where he wishes to be. He evokes that place and it comes alive, just as the animals in the museum came alive.

The mountains lie between the two different roads. A man's name passes behind the mountain's back. The road is around his place because the road curves around it. The other people's ears go to meet the returning man's names, the names he brings back. He will examine the place, for the trees of the place seem to be handsome, because they have grown tall while the man of the place, //Kabbo, has not been able to see them, has not been able to walk among them. He came to live somewhere different, somewhere that was not his place. He is the one who thinks of his place. He is the one who must return.

Their place it is not; for //Kabbo's father's father's place it was. And then it was //Kabbo's father's place when //Kabbo's father's father died. //Kabbo's eldest brother died and then it was //Kabbo's place. And then //Kabbo married when grown up, bringing !Kwabba-ang to the place, because he felt that he was alone. Therefore he grew old with his wife at the place, while he felt that his children were married.

He left Mowbray with /A!kunta on 15 October 1873. They reached Victoria West where he found his wife !Kwabba-ang who was working at the farm near the town of Vanwyksvlei, some 100 km south from Bitterpits, and this is where he remained and where he died on 25 January 1876. I don't know if he got the boots and the gun promised to him by Bleek.

XIX

3 July 2020. The cockerel died for no reason that I could see. He was well and then he was lurching around as if he was drunk and then he was dead. My neighbour said he had always been a bit odd and has replaced him with an ancient and much more friendly cockerel, decorated like a firework in a cascade of red and gold and flashes of black. He carries a fan of feathers growing at right angles from each foot and this makes him walk with a cautious and deliberate manner. He does not attack me like the other one did and he and his wives have the freedom to potter around the garden. They tend to retire to their hut and roosting perch at three in the afternoon. A simple life.

After a short absence, I have returned to the /Xam. When I visited the places where //Kabbo and his people once lived I felt very awkward in the company of their absence. I was aware of the size of my limbs, the unbending stiffness of my back, the shock in my body from the heat of the day, the effort it took for me to squat down to examine a grinding stone that had been abandoned so casually on the ground where there was once a dwelling made of branches and grasses and maybe a few spring-bok skins. It was as it was. It is as it is. I am as I am. I look at the photographs of //Kabbo and /A!kunta, the way they hold still with such a strong sense of self as the camera's eye captures them and turns them into an aspect of the history of their people that has nothing to do with their own lives and memories.

After //Kabbo and /A!kunta had set off in search of their wives, a man whose /Xam name was ‡Kasin – his Afrikaans name was Klaas Katkop – was released from the Breakwater Jail and brought to The Hill. Katkop means cat's head in Dutch and ‡Kasin's home was in the Katkop mountains, some 30 km north of the town of Brandvlei. He had been a prisoner since early 1869 after he and his brother-in-law Dia!kwain were found guilty of the culpable manslaughter of a farmer called Jakob Kruger. Lots of names here: forgive me, I cannot seem to remove them while still making sense.

This is the story. In the summer of 1868 half a dozen Trek-boer families moved north as far as a wide expanse of land south-west of Katkop. 'Beautiful rains fell and the Bushmen grass covered the plain like wheat in the wind as far as the eye could see. Game was abundant,' was how Kruger and his friends described the territory they were claiming as their own.

In those days the river still flowed for most of the year, its wide banks hemmed in by reeds and shrubs and this was where the animals of the place came to drink, to find shade, to find food. The river has been gone for a long time now and only thorn bushes are able to flourish in their own fierce manner.

The Trekboers felt they could farm here quite successfully in what they called 'these empty lands'. And so they pitched their tents and set to work preparing their new home and establishing their flocks of sheep. They were a few kilometres away from ‡Kasin and Dia!kwain's camp which lay on a hillside and above a spring that provided them with just enough water for their needs. The Bushmen group was comprised of four men, their wives and their children.

According to the evidence given by the Trekboers during the trial, some of the Bushmen visited the tents towards the end of the year. They had a gun that they might have brought with them and there was some kind of barter for which they received ammunition in return for whatever they had to barter with them. On 11 January, they came again, bringing wood which they exchanged for tobacco and sugar dumplings. Two weeks later, again according to the Trekboers, the farmer Jakob Kruger saw that six of his sheep were missing. He presumed they had been stolen by his wild neighbours.

He set off towards their camp and found a scattering of sheep bones along the way, which seemed to prove his point. As he approached the Bushmen camp, ǂKasin and his brother-in-law Dia!kwain emerged from the huts where they had been resting. They denied all knowledge of the sheep and, according to Dia!kwain, the farmer was angry and said he was going to fetch more men and then there would be serious trouble. With that he set off on his horse.

Dia!kwain's Afrikaans name was David Hoezar, or Hussar, which seems to imply that he was seen as being brave and fierce and flamboyant. He had spent his childhood close to the earlier Trekboer frontier by the Sak River and he had known a lot of violence.

His mother is said to be dead, but he does not know if this is true. They tell him the Boers killed his mother. His brothers and sisters all looked long for her but could not find her.

The Boers bound them. They drove them, making them go to the cliff. They went to lay them dead at the cliff where they had driven Kki-a-//ken and the others with horses.

Hwurri-terri who was known as Old Ruyter was brought up by the white men. He died while he was with the white men. The Boer had been beating him about herding the sheep, that he had not herded the sheep well. Therefore the Boer was beating him with the strap which people tie under their oxen's necks . . . the Boer beat him as he lay bound upon the wagon. And when the Boers thought they had done beating him a Boer unloosed him. His people came to lift him. He told them it felt as if the Boer had beaten him to death. That these people seemed to think he did not feel pain . . . He said when the Boer was beating him, he trampled on him, breaking his body's middle. This happened. The beating was the one he died of. (Dia!kwain)

According to the Boer account of what happened when Jakob Kruger turned his horse to leave, 'Lust for murder flashed in the eyes of the Bushman' and Dia!kwain shot him in the back as he rode away. ‡Kasin then took the gun and fired again, hitting the horse's saddle. Kruger managed to stay on his horse until he was within a couple of kilometres of his own people, but then he fell to the ground and the horse continued alone. By the time he was found he was already dead. He died (according to the Boer version of the story) 'so that his ancestors [sic] could live in these empty lands.'

‡Kasin and Dia!kwain fled in different directions, but they were both caught within two months. They were brought before a magistrate and much to the fury of Kruger's family and friends they were not hanged but were given the surprisingly lenient punishment of four and five years of hard labour at Breakwater Jail. ‡Kasin came to The Hill, on 1 November 1873, towards the end of his sentence. Dia!kwain arrived at the end of that same month, with another year to go. Work to be done. Stories to be collected.

Bleek's twenty-fourth notebook was eager to be filled, but ‡Kasin proved to be a bit of a disappointment. He explained that although his mother was a Bushman, his father was a Korana and that made him into what was known as a Bastard-Korana. Because of this lack of racial 'purity' Bleek was not interested in making a detailed genealogy of his family.

In his first conversation with Bleek, ‡Kasin said he understood that he needed to use his *//Khu//khuken*, his thinking strings, in order to answer the questions being put to him. He said his wife !Kweiten-ta//ken was called Rachel by the Boers. He said he had six children and he gave their names in Afrikaans. He also gave the names of his siblings, but could not remember the name of his eldest brother who was killed by a lion a long time ago. There was another older brother also known as Klaas, and one called Hans and four sisters Anntje, Kaitje, Sanna, and Mietje who died young.

‡Kasin was thought to be in his early forties. Even though he had been given his Afrikaans name because the Katkop mountains were his childhood home, you see in the two photographs of him that he has a very intense and somehow feline face. He said of himself that he used to be angry at home and once when he was hunting a jackal he came across a black snake that was as angry as he was and he ran away from its anger. In the photographs ‡Kasin could be said to look fierce, or perhaps he simply looks cornered and afraid.

He did not have many fables to tell, or maybe his fables were not considered 'pure' and so Lucy did most of the work. ‡Kasin spoke quite fluent Dutch which she translated directly into her notebook. He spoke fast, with none of //Kabbo's unfolding deliberations, so she had to write his words down very quickly in order not to lose the thread. He described his ancestral land, the plants to be found on the veld and how they were used as medicines, and as poisons for hunting.

I smear the poison on the quill.
//kururu, an insect whose poison is mixed with the poison glands of the puff adder and boomgift (tree poison), used for shooting game.
!gweh or malkopgift (bad-head poison), derived from a large root. They get a white milky looking juice from it, which they ladle into a heated, hollow stone, where it boils and becomes yellow.

Lucy showed ǂKasin a collection of dried roots, tree bark, part of a locust's legs, some powder preserved in paper and some seeds that had been found in the hut belonging to 'a Bushman sorceress'. She wrote down his account of their names and how they were used.

/hunn-ta-Oho: a piece of root from a short thick round bush, which has long roots in the ground which are dug out . . . it grows on the side of rocks. When people are ill they eat the root . . . the root is scraped into a vessel. Then boiling water is poured upon it and it is left to cool and is drunk by the sick person who is very ill . . . If only a little ill, one eats the root dry.

//kha ka O or leuuwhoud (lion wood): eaten dry when ill; also cooked in water and drunk; also burnt and applied to the temples for headaches.

!na: the lower pieces at the end of the legs of the locust . . . if one's eyes are not well, one takes the legs and sticks them into one's hair. When the eyes get better, one removes the legs and puts them by.

There was only three weeks of talk with ǂKasin, enough to fill fifty pages in four notebooks, and after that not much more to be said. When Dia!kwain arrived at the end of the month ǂKasin stepped back, remaining as a companion, but not an informant.

XX

13 July 2020. I can hear the seagull cries of children from the school playground which is what is called a stone's throw from my garden: a wonderful screeching noise that I only know is human because I know it is human. Sunshine has returned and a buzzing bee has entered the studio where I am working.

> The honeybees shall become abundant. The people bring home the honey when the sun feels hot. The people shall drink the honey liquid, sitting in the shade. (///Kabbo)

I had two emails yesterday. One from my friend Tim. It is now winter in Cape Town. The tortoises have gone quiet and are no longer fighting and mating and eating carrots; his son Adam has six teeth and is learning to crawl; there was a fire in a nearby township and he saw two whales and a shark. The nature reserve is still closed behind its high metal fences and he often thinks of the black wreck of a metal ship next to the white wreck of a whale skeleton which I saw with him when I was there.

The other email was from Paul, the photographer and one of the four of us who went to the Karoo. He had been delivering bulk supplies of food to a nearby township, but now things have become too dangerous and so he no longer goes there. He sent me a PDF of the book of photographs he made of the people he had been working with: poor and not poor, black and white, all of them staring into the camera's eye. He wondered how my book was going and if I planned to return to complete the research I had started.

I do not know the answer to that. Everywhere beyond my own immediate surroundings seems impossibly far away. Recently I bought a train ticket so I could accompany a friend to her home in the south of France and then perhaps go on to the house in the mountains in northern Italy which I still own, even though I have not seen it for almost a year. The thought of such a journey appears in my mind like that small deep window in Picasso's *Guernica*, showing that there is a world outside, even though that world feels very remote from the closed room of the present. Perhaps I will go on the train, or perhaps I will simply watch as the date of my departure moves closer and then begins to recede.

ǂKasin and Diaǃkwain were both missing their wives and children, and in March 1874 they set off on the 400-kilometre journey to the Karoo town of Calvinia in order to search for them. Bleek had been becoming increasingly frail, and with the house suddenly empty of the companionship of the /Xam, his health went into a sharp decline and he started coughing blood. He wrote to Sir George Grey about the approach of mortality: 'For my children and for the completion of many important works begun, I wish much to live on; but feel every year that this may not entirely depend upon one's wishes; and that the end may be nearer at hand than one has any idea of.'

Just three months after their departure, ǂKasin and Diaǃkwain made an unexpected return to Mowbray. Diaǃkwain was without his family, but ǂKasin was accompanied by two of his four surviving children and his wife ǃKweiten-ta-//ken, who was Diaǃkwain's sister and whose name meant orphan's child. Maybe they had come because they were afraid of reprisals from the friends of the farmer they had killed, or maybe it was simply too difficult to find a way to survive in their own country now that it no longer belonged to them. By some curious coincidence, Bleek's health improved almost at once when they were back in the house, and he again began to record some of Dia!kwain's memories and had a rather prurient interview with ǂKasin in July in which he asked more questions about sexual organs, and the sexual act: 'On the side . . . his thighs. The man lies with his front towards the woman's back he . . . her buttocks . . . his belly.'

!Kweiten-ta-//ken was unhappy and homesick. She was not interviewed by Bleek, but Lucy spent a week trying to talk to her. She told of the maiden who killed the water's children and was turned into a frog; of the man who cut open his wife's belly because she was too fat and then found out that she was pregnant; of the man who cut off his own thigh and of the leopard tortoise who asked several men to rub her neck with fat and their hands became trapped within her shell. But the telling was brief and filled only two of Lucy's notebooks. In January 1875 !Kweiten-ta-//ken and her husband ǂKasin and the children set off north to the Karoo and there is no way of knowing what happened to them.

Dia!kwain stayed on. 'My life here is a little bit nice,' he once said to Lucy. He was gentle and kind to Jemima's daughters and he seemed to play a stabilising role within this family of women, all of them watching over Bleek and fearful of what might come next.

In February the household moved into a property called Charlton House. Lucy had by now taken on most of the responsibility for collecting information from Dia!kwain, while Bleek kept himself busy with his earlier and more abstracted task of completing a Bushman–English dictionary and a comparative grammar of South African languages. He clearly felt he was living on borrowed time and was concerned that his life's work on the language and culture of a people on the edge of extinction should not itself disappear without trace.

Lucy went on working steadily with Dia!kwain, as death moved closer to her brother-in-law. She learned that he was brought up close to a place called !Kann where there was a spring of water from which they drank, and before the time of the Boers his father scratched images of gemsbok, quagga and ostriches onto the black surface of the volcanic boulders that once poured out of the earth's core, but then stood still.

The second of his three sisters was /A-kumm, Story of a Fight. The third sister was Whai-ttu, Springbok Skin, although she was known as Griet by the Boers. He believed his mother was dead; killed by the Boers.

He spoke of his childhood: of insects, edible roots, the hive of bees his grandfather showed him, the locusts his mother warned him not to play with, her collection of European needles. He described the musical instruments of the /Xam, including the !goin-!goin whose name sounds like the powerful range of echoing musical notes that resounded from the split sides of some of the dolerite boulders when you hit them with a round stone. He told of people dancing, the men calling out like male ostriches and the women clapping their hands in reply.

From Dia!kwain came the story of the girl who drank the lioness's milk and the story of the lion who licked the tears of the man he thought was dead. But whatever he said was overshadowed by the memory of the terrible violence he had witnessed and that now he kept remembering in this house where the white man was gravely ill.

He remembered a massacre in which:

The men all lay dead. And he saw the Boers must have been those that killed the men, therefore the men returned not on account of it. A woman said, 'You shall leave sheep's fat for the white breasted crow, because the white breasted crow told the truth when he came to tell us nicely that all our menfolk are murdered.'

Two weeks before Bleek's death, Dia!kwain spoke of his father Xaa-ttin, who was a man of great spiritual power. He told Lucy that Xaa-ttin wanted to pass on what he knew to his son before he died. He said that the world he inhabited had changed almost beyond recognition: nothing was as it once had been and what he called 'the string', which used to connect the people with 'the ringing sound in the sky', had been broken. In telling of this loss, Dia!kwain sang his words, to echo that ringing sound which was no longer heard.

> The place became like this to me, because the string broke for me. Therefore the place does not feel to me as the place used to feel for me. The place does not feel pleasant to me because the string was broken.
>
> My father sang that the string had broken, the string he used to hear when his father called upon the Rain Bull. Now I do not hear the ringing sound in the sky which I used to hear. I feel that the string has broken and gone away from me. Therefore when I sleep I do not feel any thing which vibrates in me while I sleep. For when I was asleep I used to hear a thing, as if a person called me.

With that I am brought back to the memory of my husband when he was at his most frail during a harsh cancer treatment. He was sitting in a wheelchair in the hospital gardens when he said, 'I feel as if my soul is attached to my body by the thinnest silver thread,' and for a moment I could see the thread, stretching up into the sky.

XXI

Early days of August. The continuity of sunshine. I drive to a familiar place and from there I walk a familiar path to the sea. There is a point where the clustering shelter of oak woods comes to an abrupt end and I am led into an expanse of reed beds, beneath an enormous sky. In the past I have always found that the transition from the enclosure of the trees to the openness of the reeds would shift whatever mood I was in by surrounding me with a sense of the celebration of the beauty of the world. But now it is different. The glinting light on reeds and on pools of water is as powerful as ever, but I do not see it with the old clarity because I am, as it were, beside myself. We are all beside ourselves: impatiently trapped within the present moment, but nervous of the future, which is close but out of sight; a lion sleeping in a cave perhaps, since August is the month of the lion. I think I can hear it breathing in the darkness.

In a parallel time in the early days of August 1875, while Wilhelm Bleek's body laboured to stay alive, Dia!kwain told Lucy of a dream that spoke to him, 'just as if a person had spoken.'

I dreamt that father and I were cutting up a sheep. The Boer came up to us as we were cutting it up and said he would beat us to death. The dream spoke to me this that I told the Boer not to kill us at once, but to let us work for him, instead of killing us.

I did not want him to kill my father. I wanted to work out what my father owed for the sheep. I would work out both what I owed and what my father owed.

And the dream said to me that I saw my father lying dead in the sun's heat. And I wept when I thought that I saw that my father really had died. And I asked the Boer, did he think it was such a big thing that we had killed, that he acted thus? He should have let us work it out and not acted as he did.

Dia!kwain woke and recounted the dream to his wife and by now the wind had changed direction and was coming from the north, bringing gathering clouds and a dust storm and the promise of rain that was also part of the dream.

He said they returned home to where they lived with a Boer farmer and two days later his mother came to visit them with the news that his father had really died. She said the death was caused by the pain in his back which he had often complained about, but I can't help wondering if the pain was itself the result of a beating. There was always so much violence.

Dia!kwain's mother told him how the springbok had behaved in a strange way when Xaa-ttin died.

Mother did not know where the springbok came from. They were not few. They came and played, as they approached the hut where father lay dead. They appeared to be moving away and the wind really blew, following them.

The closeness of talk between Dia!kwain and Lucy continued, and on 11 August, the day before my birthday and just six days before Bleek's death, he told her how a mist can descend on the people, trying to help them when they are caught in a predicament of desperation and danger. This was what he said happened when a group of them were attacked by the Boers.

At the time when the people have come near to attack us, at the time when they intend to reach us, it is morning, the mist sits there, our mist. They shoot at us in the mist.

We make clouds. Our blood is smoking, while we feel that the mist is that in which the people are shooting us. Therefore we make clouds, when the people have come to us . . . and when the people went away . . . the mist also went, while it felt that our blood had flowed out.

On 16 August Bleek caught a severe cold and his lungs failed him and he was haemorrhaging blood: 'while it felt that our blood had flowed out.'

On 17 August he seemed very bright and happy and was busy sorting through the words in the Bushman dictionary, so Lucy could begin pasting on the sheets, in readiness for printing just as soon as the necessary funds had been found. That evening he played with the children, but felt tired and went to bed early.

His wife Jemima was five months pregnant and the family situation was extremely precarious, but it seems that all the Lloyd sisters had a natural resilience. In a long letter to Sir George Grey, Jemima described her husband's final hours:

When I went to our room that night at quarter to eleven, he was already in bed but still awake and spoke to me occasionally both while I was putting ready the little comforts he might want during the night and also several times after I put out my candle at eleven and lay down beside him, seeming quite as well as usual.

But then before either of us had fallen asleep a want of power in moving his right arm attracted attention and I spoke to him but received no answer. Striking a light I saw he was awake and looking at me and that he tried to speak but could not . . . a sort of wondering, half puzzled look came into his eyes and then a very sweet smile, but he never visibly tried to speak again.

In that same letter, Jemima spoke of her husband as 'my dear lion' as if he, just like the /Xam whose lives had intertwined so closely with his, had acquired the power to transform himself into the shape of another creature.

> Grandfather !Nwin/kuiten used to become a lion . . . he got a Boer's ox, while he was a lion. He killed a Boer's ox. The Boer called together a commando against him. The Boer went to shoot him. He told my father about it . . . he knew not whether my father would see him again, but the thing seemed as if he should die . . . For a Boer really had shot him . . . He spoke to my father of the pain which he suffered, that father might know he was suffering. Things felt as if he must soon go and leave him. He had desired to teach my father his magic which he worked, then father would know the things he had taught him and would not forget them. (Dai!kwain)

An obituary in the *Cape Argus* spoke of 'the cultural intellect of the earnest, big-browed German' and went on to mention that a 'semi-savage . . . with his pigmy stature and prognathous dusky face' was at his master's side. Perhaps Dia!kwain was there in the bedroom of the dying man as a witness and a guide.

Shortly after his death, Bleek's youngest daughter told Dia!kwain that an owl had flown close to her window in the night, frightening her. He was pleased with the news. He said the owl was her father who had come to see that she was all right.

XXII

19 August 2020. Time has been and gone. My son was here with his family and his wife's parents stayed in a house across the road and I was wrapped up in talk and laughter; the little ones riding on my back or being lifted in my arms, scrambling over me early in the morning while I lay in bed. Then my daughter and her husband and their daughter came for my birthday and stayed until the day before her birthday and they set up their tent on a campsite close to the sea and we ate sausages cooked on a wood stove and sat in a heap on a big blow-up mattress and the dog sat with us and their daughter was brave enough to come and stay with me for two nights on her own and I could not help interrupting the sweetness of the present moments by wishing that time would hold its breath just a little longer.

My five-year-old granddaughter wanted to know about the death of my husband and what happened and did I mind him dying. I told her he died in this garden and I miss him a lot but I did not mind, because he did not mind; he felt too old to go on living and she seemed to find that a good answer.

When the moon stood hollow, mother said, 'the moon is carrying people who are dead . . . A person has died when it lies in this way.' (Dia!kwain)

My six-year-old granddaughter told me she has frightening dreams which she cannot remember, and when we slept together in the same bed she began to thrash like a fish out of water with the first light of the dawn, presumably because of the dreams. During the day she often walked around the garden cradling a chicken in her arms and the chicken learned to wait for her, crouching down at her feet in the hope of being picked up again.

> Mother took a stone and thrust the stone into the fire's ashes because she wished the bad things of which she had been dreaming should altogether go in the fire and that they should not walk with her. (Dia!kwain)

Now they have all gone and I have put the exhausted French beans and sweet peas onto the compost heap. Most of the perpetual spinach is shooting woody stems that hold tiny and inedible leaves. The broccoli plants are huge and not much bothered by caterpillars. A friend of a friend offered me the custody of a spur-thighed tortoise, said to be almost a hundred years old. I have always wanted a tortoise, but although I spoke to the friend of the friend and saw a photograph of the tortoise sitting on a woolly jumper, I must have failed the interview because I have heard no more. I think I would have worried during the months of hibernation in case the sleep of death was taking over. I know you can put a tortoise in the fridge during the winter and I do have an empty fridge that might have been just right for the purpose, or not. Uncertainty is in the air. The virus is beginning to return to the countries it seemed to have left.

Wilhelm Bleek is dead. His four daughters and his wife and her three sisters are all living under the one roof and they are all in mourning for their loss. Dia!kwain was in many ways the head of the household and he took his responsibilities very seriously, but still he missed his wife and his own family. By now he had been here for seven months with none of his own people to keep him company; or, as Bleek put it, 'no chattering like a monkey with his friends'.

On 20 August he dictated a letter to his sister Whai-ttu which Lucy wrote down in a rather flowery English as well as in /Xam, sending it to the farm where he thought she was living, but there was no reply.

> Why can it be that !Kweiten-ta-//ken and her family do not send me a letter, that I might hear whether they have gone to the place to which they returned . . . they must allow me to know why it is that they do not seem as if they remember me, that they do not speak to me . . .
>
> I had now intended to return. My master, he was the one who told me that I should first wait a little, as he did not yet desire that I should return and go away from him, for I had thought to return. He, in August's moon . . . died, leaving us.
>
> Therefore I know not what I shall do about it, for my mistress is still weeping. That is why I am still sitting melancholy on account of it . . . for I am still looking at my mistress. For I do not yet wish to go away from my mistress, while she is still weeping . . .

As part of his wish to help Lucy by sharing his own experiences of loss, Dia!kwain told her of the death of his first wife Mietje.

> When the sun was setting my wife died. We waited for her sister's child to come and buried her when she came and we slept at home and the springbok came that night to see the place at which we had buried my wife. These things are those we do not speak of. We will remain silent.

On the day after Mietje's burial, he and his sister and a number of others saw a figure who looked like a little child sitting with crossed legs on the white expanse of a salt pan, and it seemed to be wearing the same cap that his wife always wore. Whai-ttu said 'the thing resembles my brother's wife' and it watched them as they walked away.

His wife had a baby girl, but he had to leave it to be nursed by his other sister, and then a year or so later he took a second wife who bore him two sons and it was this family that he was now missing. He was anxious to find them again and perhaps to obtain news of his sons who he believed were working for Boer farmers, but he did not know where.

You can see the quietness of Dia!kwain in the two photographs taken during this time, along with what appears like a confiding quality. Lucy was forty by now and he was just ten years her junior and the two of them clearly had a very easy relationship of talk and trust.

His stories of all the savagery and injustice that he and //Kabbo and the others had seen must have been in Lucy's mind when she wrote a letter to a female acquaintance, saying what she had learned from:

Bushmen who lived with us at Mowbray, with regard to the treatment received by them from the generality of farmers. For instance, that their waterpits were taken from them, although they had belonged to certain Bushman families for generations; that the game had been driven from their hunting grounds; that the ostrich whom they seem to look upon as a possession and to kill with a certain reserve and consideration, and whose eggs and flesh contributed greatly to their maintenance were chased to death by the farmers on horseback in the hot sun and left dead and wasting on the ground, of no use to anyone, not having been killed by the farmers for food . . . There are few things which I would more gladly do than endeavour to make the acquaintance of the Bushmen in their own homes. I fear, however, that one would be likely to see a good deal that would give much heartache, without the power to make things better.

In March 1876 Dia!kwain finally left Charlton House and went north in search of his people, a place to be, a way of living. He promised to return if he could.

It is known that he worked for a while at a farm in Calvinia and then he set off into the country with another /Xam man, going from farm to farm and visiting his sister to see if he could hear news of his sons. They reached a farm that was incongruously called Klavervlei or Clover Marsh, belonging to one Nicolaas Louw, and this was where his wife Johanna was staying, but still he would not stop his restless journey. He accompanied Louw as far as Kenhardt, and then continued on his own into the Orange Free State. Finally he looped back to Kenhardt.

An owl made Dia!kwain's sister La-kkum think that danger was at hand when she came from !Kau-/nunu. The white men's houses were not yet at Kenhardt, for the Bushmen were those who inhabited that place.

The news of his presence was quickly picked up by the Boer farmers of the region and they were eager to revenge the death of Jakob Kruger. And so they banded together and murdered the man called Dia!kwain.

XXIII

21 August 2020. A fierce wind is blowing. The Arctic ice is melting so fast that I keep forgetting just how fast, probably because I want to hold such knowledge at bay. Our prime minister is believed to be on holiday in a tent. He has not made a public announcement for weeks, although he did say we must try to avoid what he called the atomic bomb of another countrywide lockdown and God only knows what he meant by that. He remained silent on the day when the destruction of Hiroshima and Nagasaki were being remembered; maybe he was not taught at school about what an atomic bomb does to those who stand in its way.

I turn to the man called /Han‡kass'o, known also by his Afrikaans name of Kleine Jaantje, or Little Johnny, because //Kabbo was Oude Jantje and he was //Kabbo's son-in-law.

> /Han‡kass'o's mother's father was the one killed with the rhinoceros horn. His father's father was Tsoa!e whom the lion killed at night. The lion comes. The lion grasps him at night.

He was photographed several times in 1878. In one image he is shown in profile and bare-chested and you see him as the skilled hunter he once was, staring out at the far distance of another world where ostrich, kudu, eland and the great herds of spring-bok are crowding across the land.

In a very different photograph he is gazing straight at the camera's eye. Now he is sitting on a chair covered with fur, fox fur perhaps. He is wearing a huge jacket which almost envelops him, a check shirt and hot-looking trousers, and he is holding a bow very delicately in his elegant hands. A measuring rod emerges incongruously from the side of his jacket as if it had been put there like a bamboo cane to support a growing plant, but presumably it was intended to provide more technical information for Mr Huxley's studies of the physiognomy of the savage races. You see sadness and something like resignation in his beautiful face, but you also see an authority which makes him appear, to me at least, like a king from an ancient Egyptian dynasty.

/Han≠kass'o was one of the group arrested and imprisoned with //Kabbo and the rest of the so-called Tooren Gang. He was married to //Kabbo's daughter Suobba-//ken and his convict number was 4630, although there is no description of him in the Description Register of the Breakwater Jail. He first came to stay with the Bleek family in June 1871, but he was not interviewed and he was sent off to Bushmanland in November of that same year to see if he could find //Kabbo's wife and bring her back to Mowbray. He finally returned after a seven-year absence and that was when he told Lucy the story of his early life and the tragedies that came later.

In February 1876 /Han≠kass'o heard that //Kabbo had died at the farm of Vanwyksvlei which was where he had been living all this time, since he could never go back to his home at Bitterpits. /Han≠kass'o and his wife Suobba-//ken went there to look after his mother-in-law !Kwabba-ang and to go through the traditional period of mourning with her. She died quite suddenly in March of the following year and so in April he and Suobba-//ken began the long journey to Mowbray, taking their baby with them, but leaving their son !Hun !hun with friends.

They got as far as the town of Beaufort West and this is where Suobba-//ken was beaten so badly by a policeman that she died a few days later. The baby also died at around the same time. /Han-ǂkass'o went on alone and arrived in Mowbray in January 1878. There were no /Xam staying in the house and so Lucy tried to arrange for his son to join them, but !Hun !hun had been inden-tured (if that is the right word for the absolute ownership of a human being) to a farmer who wouldn't let him go, even though Lucy did her best to persuade him.

So there he was, bereft of all family and with none of his peo-ple with him and yet wanting to speak, to add his voice to the voices of //Kabbo and Dia!kwain and the others. Maybe he also wanted to have a quiet time after so much trouble. The Bleek children remembered that he played ball with them and gave them presents he had carved out of wood: a tiny bow and arrows, a doll's chair, the musical instrument known as a !goin !goin. He was a skilled storyteller and they could follow the drama of what he was saying even though they could not understand the words, as his protagonists spoke in the language of the baboon – 'the people who sit upon their heels' – the ostrich, the jackal, hyena and anteater, the sounds they articulated somehow relating to the particular shape and position of the mouth. His stories also con-tained crying and whispering, whimpering and moaning. He sang songs. He danced. He became the owner of a kitten which could not walk properly and he named Kauki, 'the one who does not hear'. And yet at the same time he was a grave and solemn man filled with sadness.

Lucy took him to the museum and he knew a lot about insects in particular. This is what he said about the withered leaf insect:

We clap our hands at it. It nods its head while we say, 'Oh withered leaf insect, up, up, up go!' While we wish that it should nod its head . . . We clap our hands while we feel that our elders were those who did thus. Therefore we who are children clap our hands to the withered leaf insect.

During his childhood /Hanǂkass'o was very close to his maternal grandfather Tsatsi. 'I used to sleep with my grandfather. I sat with my grandfather when he sat in the cool outside. Therefore I questioned him about the things which spoke thus.' Tsatsi taught him how to make fire with two sticks, how to make poison with snake venom and the juice from a certain plant, how to make bows and arrows, how to hunt the porcupine and about the stars.

Just like all his people, /Hanǂkass'o spoke of hunger and cruelty and the loss of an entire world. In quite a matter-of-fact way he told Lucy of the poverty of the Bushmen and how if a white man gives them a piece of fat, they render it and pour it 'on a dish, an ostrich dish, and they bring a tortoise shell and they set it down

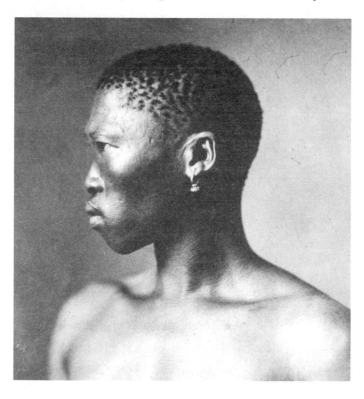

/Hanǂkass'o

135

and they take a spoon of springbok or sheep horn and they ladle this fat upon the tortoise shell . . . and they take the fat which is here, while they feel that they are an orphaned (poor) people, therefore they divide the fat into small quantities.'

While still young, he went to live with //Kabbo's people at the Bitterpits and there he was in much closer proximity to the white farmers. It seems he kept moving on from one farm to another, explaining that 'there are two farmers only in his part of the country who are good to the Bushmen and who do not drive them away from the water.' He spoke of a woman called Doortje who worked for the farmer Jakob de Klerk and his wife Trina. The farmer's wife punished Doortje after she broke a cup she was washing up.

Doortje became insensible because the Mistress had been beating her. The Mistress stood upon her, the Mistress trampled her, and she, when the wind was cold, she became cool. We lifted her up. We put her in the house while she breathed not. And the place became dark as she lay, while she could not breathe.

The farmer often beat Doortje as well, using 'a reed that is large. It is the one to which the people say //hui !ka ka !nwa, the reed the white man calls Bamboo', and after one of these beatings she could no longer see well.

They do not think that we are people who feel pain.

Just as //Kabbo had been able to walk back in his mind to the place of his ancestors, the bee honeycombs, the tall trees, the bitter water, his wife and children waiting for him, so too when /Han‡kass'o spoke of hunting he stepped into a past time in which the springbok were like the stars of the Milky Way and he could practise his skill and knowledge as a hunter of these beautiful animals that had, as it were, agreed to be killed, so that he and his family might live.

> We go behind the hill for the springbok are coming. The springbok are so numerous the bushes are not to be seen because of them, for it is the springbok bodies which are coming. The dust is arising, on account of them.

He slings on his quiver, the arrows 'rattling along, rattling along'. He makes a shelter of bushes by night and lies down there. He goes to sit in a place while he feels 'that these springbok footpaths are those that the springbok intend to take.' The women are waiting until the sun is warm; the children are driving the spring-bok forward 'while the place is still cold', and /Han‡kass'o is ready and waiting.

> The mother springbok when she trots along, when she has a springbok child which is little, she grunts as she trots along. She grunts when the child plays. She says a a a a a as she trots along, making a sound while the springbok feel that they are numerous. Her children also make a sound. Their mothers say a a a a a, the children say me me me me me . . . The people say that the springbok resemble the Milky Way. They also say the springbok resemble the stars.

> I sit here. The male springbok are those which will go by, passing behind me. I cough, imitating the springbok. And they, while they feel that I am lying down, they do not perceive me. They go passing behind me. The old rams are those which go forward, calling, grunting and lowing as they go in among the springbok mothers as the spring-bok which the women have startled, come.

There were several ways of hunting the springbok and it was sometimes done with the aid of ostrich feathers attached to sticks

4. This man whose sticks they are, lies at
   their head.
5.⎤ See VIII. ——   pp.
6.⎥
7.⎦

4. 𝛾   𝛾
   𝛾
        8

            7

         6

1   2

1. From this direction the herd   3
   of springbok comes
2. Here they go towards the row of
   sticks with feathers tied upon them.
3. Here stands a woman, who throws up dust into the air.
       Row of sticks with feathers tied upon
   them, used in springbok-hunting, to turn the
   same. The lines represent the Bushmen lines

138

and stuck in the ground at regular intervals, their whiteness, their blackness and their dizzy energy waving in the wind. The springbok are afraid of the feather bushes and to avoid the feathers, they run to where the hunters lie in wait for them.

/Han‡kass'o made a drawing to show how the technique worked and Lucy added her own explanatory notes on the page.

1. From this direction the herd comes.
2. Here they go towards the row of sticks with feathers tied upon them.
3. Here stands the woman who throws dust into the air.
4. The man who is the leader of the hunt.
5. This man, he has ostrich feathers upon sticks.
6. He wants to look like a man who stands, so that the springbok may see it when they go towards the lesser feather bushes. For the springbok would otherwise, turning back, pass behind him, while he was driving the springbok for the other people.
7. He also sticks in a little feather brush which is short, to drive the springbok, that the foremost may run.
8. Passing by the man who lies between.

From /Han‡kass'o comes the story of the man who threw dust into the sky so that the people could see him when he could no longer walk because the heat of the day was killing him.

He sits up to remove the darkness from his face, for the sun's darkness resembles night.

From him also comes 'in the mouth of coolness', the greeting that people gave to each other in the early evening, and the story of a man who was dying after he accidentally wounded himself with his own poisoned arrow, and the people wanted to cut out the wounded area to try to bleed the poison away, but he would not let them because this was the place where he knew he must die, 'my heart stands in the hill', he said.

Lucy tried to find companions for /Han‡kass'o, but when she thought she had arranged for a /Xam family to come to Mowbray, they proved to be Korana Hottentots with whom no communication was possible.

She then arranged for two young !Kun Bushman boys from the part of Namibia close to the Olifants River to be brought to live with them. The boys had been abducted and sold and sold again, and when they first arrived in September 1879, they were silent and traumatised. /Han‡kass'o was able to play what she called 'a fatherly role with them', but they were not his people and he could not communicate with them or find the comfort of shared memories.

And so in December 1879 he left Mowbray and set off in search of his son !Hun !hun. It is known that he made his way safely to the town of Kenhardt some twenty kilometres north from the place where he was born, but there the trail comes to an end.

XXIV

27 August 2020. Autumn has rushed in as if from nowhere, and the runner beans I wrapped up in plastic bags to keep them safe from a cold spring night have completed their cycle. I pulled them up and dumped them in a heap with the other plants that have served a brief purpose. It is so long since I have grown any vegetables that I forgot the fact of the seasons and the changes they bring.

I am beginning to feel that this book is becoming a book. There is still a lot to be done but it seems to know where it is going, or at least the direction it needs to take. When I get stuck I turn to the short pieces I have copied out from the /Xam texts and I read them aloud in the silence of this studio where I sit and work. I had thought to transform them into a series of independent poems to serve as a sort of postscript at the end, but I've given up on that idea and if they don't fit within these pages, then I must let them go.

Having got this far I stop for a moment to walk out into the garden and there is a rabbit crouched in the grass a couple of yards away from me, overwhelmed by the myxoma virus and trying to wash its red and swollen eyes with its paws. It must have sensed my presence because it slowly blunders into the protection of some bushes.

I go back to my desk and start to write about the four boys of the !Kun Bushman group who came to stay at Charlton House between 1879 and 1881. They had a shared language, although each one of them came from a slightly different area in north-east Namibia: thin and frightened children swept up in the storm of the time they were living in.

For we seemed to think that being an orphan is a light thing, but a great thing it is.

!Nanni (top left), /Uma (middle), Tamme (right) and Da

Two of the boys had seen their parents murdered. All of them had been stolen and bartered, forgotten and lost and found again, until finally the first two and then the other two were put on a boat called the *Louis Alfred* and taken down the coast from Walvis Bay and round to the port in Cape Town. From there they were delivered to Lucy Lloyd like little parcels, and for a while they stayed with her and all the others at Charlton House. And then they were gone, back into the storm.

When they arrived, these boys were almost speechless from the traumas they had gone through, so Lucy needed to find a way of approaching them and learning their language and their stories. Previously Dia!kwain and /Han‡kass'o had added to their narratives by making beautiful drawings of the creatures they were describing, and /Han‡kass'o had also provided the diagram of the ostrich-feather trap for the springbok. Now Lucy realised that the children might be able to communicate in pictures all the things that they could not say in words. And so she provided them with paper and pencils and paint and even red clay, and from these materials they began to depict the world that they had known and then they were ready to speak of what they had made visible. Lucy was quick to learn their language and their words eventually filled over a thousand pages in her notebooks.

Da, the youngest child, was only six when he arrived, but all four of them were able to produce extraordinary images of flowers and fruits, of bulbs and roots, and trees big enough for an entire boat to be carved from a single trunk. Here were elephants and ostriches and lions, antelope, small rodents and insects and so many birds, and often the children placed the plant or fruit that a particular creature liked to eat somewhere close by. There were also drawings of the people of other races who had captured them as they made their slow journey to Cape Town, and maps of the country in which they had lived and of the layout of the little dwelling places that had once been home.

The boys spoke as they worked, *it is on the earth in my country, it is abundant in my country*, but just as with //Kabbo when he re-entered the memory of his life at Bitterpits to which he could never return, or /Han‡kass'o when he relived the experience of hunting the animals that no longer came to the ancestral hunting grounds, these children were remembering birds and animals that had ceased to be abundant; plants and trees that no longer grew with such profusion on the veld or close to the banks of the river.

The first European missionaries had arrived in the country now called Namibia in the mid 1850s. They were followed by a handful of hunters, several of whom metamorphosed into trad-ers, explorers and mining prospectors. Beyond the barrier of the Namib Desert lay Damaraland, a desert region north and south of the Okavango River which was transformed into lush grass-lands and marshes during the rainy season, attracting quantities of wildlife. Within two decades of its discovery by the Europeans, the area had been pretty much stripped to the bone. A hunter/trader called Eriksson remembered that in a single year in the late 1870s he had collected more than three thousand elephant tusks in Damaraland.

> The word ivory rang in the air, was whispered, was sighed. You would think they were praying to it. A taint of imbe-cile rapacity blew through it all, like a whiff from some corpse. (Joseph Conrad, *Heart of Darkness*)

Ten years later, all Eriksson could find were the tracks of a single female and her calf and the tracks of one old bull.

Once the supply of ivory had dried up, the trade in guns, the sale and acquisition of cattle and the theft and sale of young chil-dren, became the new currency. Rival groups fought each other to the death, and for communities such as the !Kun Bushmen there was nowhere safe to live and nothing much to live on now that the wild animals and the natural vegetation were being replaced by arid pastures for livestock. As our friend Eriksson said, 'Berg Damara [Bushmen] are starving, my store is breeched from morning to night with living skeletons.'

With my notes heaped across the table, I tried to race as fast as I could through this story of destruction because I could not bear to look at it in too much detail; just as I cannot bear to look at the faces of certain politicians, cannot bear to look at the photograph of a catch of huge and strange fish heaved up by fishermen from the waters around the Galapagos Islands; cannot bear to think of the melting ice of the polar ice caps, or the melting glaciers in the mountain regions of northern Italy that have changed so much in the twenty years that I have known them. And then because of my nervousness I somehow managed to delete an almost complete chapter in the moment when I thought I was saving it, and no amount of clicking or searching would bring it back to life.

The next day I went to London to look after my eldest grand-daughter and time passed in playing hide-and-seek in the park and eating ice cream and watching films that left me spinning from the dizzy speed of the action, and when I got back all that I could resuscitate from my lost chapter was a timeline and a list.

The timeline followed the development of gun technology, as the art of killing with speed and efficiency from a safe distance was improved.

1853: the musket replaced by the Enfield rifle, effective at a range of 500 yards and firing much more quickly.

1869: Enfields replaced by the Martini-Henry: faster and more accurate, insensitive to damp and jolts. The French had the Gras rifle, the Prussians had the Mauser.

1871–2: Henry Morton Stanley apparently inspected an early model of the Maxim gun and was very impressed by what it could do, saying it would be of *valuable service in helping civilization to overcome barbarism.*

1885: repeater mechanisms introduced. By the end of the

1890s, you could shoot lying down in all weathers, fifteen shots in fifteen seconds at a distance of a thousand yards.

The list was simply an inventory of the goods imported to Eriksson's trading station in Damaraland in 1878; which happens to be the same year in which the four !Kun boys were taken from their homes.

1000 rifles
9070 kg gunpowder
8165 kg tobacco
1818 litres gin
2726 litres of brandy
726 kg rice
17963 kg coffee
23134 kg sugar
1769 kg tea
5453 litres lager
2268 kg wax
4536 kg soap
2722 kg other goods.

XXV

7 September 2020. Quite early this morning I started reading one of my many notebooks. This one is black and postcard-sized and it has 2011 and 2013 roughly scrawled in Tipp-Ex on the cover.

In October 2011 I was trying to decide what I might write next, reassuring myself that if I couldn't write anything for a while, then I could make jam, or hem a curtain, or plant the narcissi bulbs.

In that same month I found a plump and perplexed little auk washed up on the beach of Walberswick in Suffolk, and by November I was at the Venice Biennale, but I only mentioned the work in the Polish Pavilion: *a big video installation showing a young man standing in an overgrown amphitheatre and crying out, 'Come home, Jews, we need you! Come home, the three million!'*

I made a note that according to Socrates a thing is not seen because it is visible, but visible because it is seen, and then there is a jump in time and it's suddenly January 2013 and I recorded a dream of being by a river with my daughter and perhaps my husband was there as well, but I wasn't sure. I had forgotten the dream until now.

On the next page I quoted from a letter that the physician, artist and ornithologist Edward Wilson wrote to his wife in 1912, as he lay dying in the tent with Scott and the others on that expedition to the South Pole. 'God knows,' he says, 'I am sorry to be the cause of sorrow to anyone in the world, but everyone must die and at every death there must be some sorrow . . . I feel so happy now in having got time to write to you . . . All is well.'

A list of wild flowers followed: 'eyebright and speedwell, lousewort and broomrape, sheep-bit and bellflower'; and then the notebook came to an end with a short poem by Ezra Pound:

> And the days are not full enough
> And the nights are not full enough
> And life slips by like a field mouse
> Not shaking the grass.

It all feels so long ago; another life, another time, and here I am here and it's 9 September 2020 and I am still struggling to tell a story which is similar to the story of the /Xam in the Karoo, except that these are young children, being asked to explain who they are and what they have seen and where they once belonged.

!Nanni and Tamme were the first to arrive. They were brought by William Coates Palgrave, who knew that Lucy wanted to learn the !Kun language and thought this might be a good way to do it. Palgrave has what looks like a friendly face beneath a big beard. Between 1876 and 1885 he was the Cape Colony's commissioner to Namibia, with the job of assessing 'the resources of the country and the disposition of various tribes . . . explaining to them the benefits and advantages they would derive from Colonial Rule.' He was involved in several other governmental tasks.

Anyway, Palgrave and his big beard handed the first two boys over to Lucy in the Company's Gardens in the centre of Cape Town and she set to work immediately, leading them up the white marble steps and into the Museum of Natural History. Together they walked between the heavy glass cabinets with their displays of dead animals and dead birds and insects, and once again she asked for the names of the silent creatures that stared out from their strange imprisonment. That was a beginning of sorts, and then off they went to the house in the village of Mowbray: a serious and pale Englishwoman in her early forties along with two thin and frightened children from the north-east of Namibia.

!Nanni was the older of the two and was thought to be in his late teens, although he looks much younger. In the photographs he appears more resolute than Tamme, less terrified. He said his home was by 'a great water' and he lived there with his mother and other people. And then he made two maps: one of his country and one of his home.

Using a thin pencil he drew the line of a river which was called //Xumm by his people. He said it only flowed for a few weeks during the rainy season and that was when the elephants came, following the muddy riverbed on heavy feet.

The elephant killed my mother's sister at night. My mother's sister was alone. The elephant were numerous. My mother's sister died. My mother cried, cried. My mother was silent.

He marked permanent pools of water enclosed by reeds and rushes. There were many trees, he said, some very big.

On one side of the river he drew the road belonging to the people known as the Dama, and the European Road was just beneath it, often drifting close to the pools of water. He drew the Bushman Road which led into Bushman Country, a place of many fruit trees, and he drew what he called Elephant Country where there were thorn trees and waterholes. Another European Road crossed over the river from the land of the Dama and set off parallel to the Bushman Road, continuing down into Makoba Country. It also looped back on itself in order to visit more pools of water where the animals came in such numbers to drink.

!Nanni's other map showed a group of circles that were five

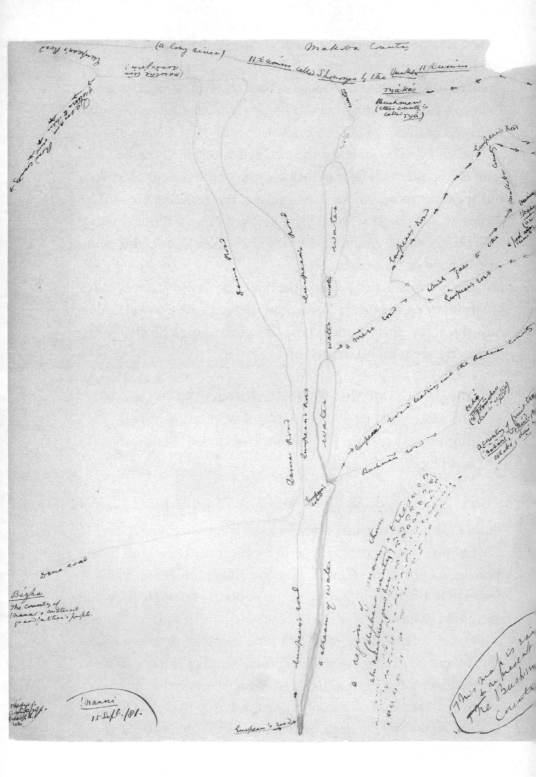

huts. Here was his mother's hut, his father's hut, the huts of his grandfather Kanu and of his brother and of himself. Each hut had a star shape in front of it: a little fire that was always kept burning, to keep what Dia!kwain called 'the thing which walks at night' at bay. A cross-hatched line was a longer fire where meat, fruit and vegetables were cooked. A circle marked with three dots represented the body of his sister who died and he and his brother sat outside his brother's hut to weep for her. Near that place was another circle which was the mound of earth surrounded by little fires, under which she was buried. A circle with three dots in it, enclosed by a second circle, was the grave of his grandfather Kanu, who looked after him when his parents were away and had taught him everything he needed to know about being a !Kun Bushman.

> We do not throw away our old man. Our old person takes nicely care of us. Our mother goes out. She seeks other food. Our mother gathers something. Our old person keeps us in the hut.

From Kanu !Nanni learned that a lion must always be respected, and he made a diagram of the house of a Bushman who was afraid of a lion: a sort of cartwheel with spokes coming out of it that I like to think are the man's fear. Kanu said that when a man dies, his things are not given to another man because this would make his wife cry, and he explained the way the people prepared the corpse.

> The man's father should be the one to dress and arrange the dead man's body. The dead man should be dressed with a male jackal's skin . . . His head should rest on his bag and he should wear two jackal's ears as bracelets, with the feet of the jackal hung upon his head.

11. on ta'le Thâru   13.
12. stones (large)
13. Thâru tchû 13.2, Hâru's fire.
14. stones (small)
15. grass-mouth (closed)

16. Thâridson Bō
hause. 16.2, his
fire

16·a.   16.

'nanni. 22 Jany /80.

1. umim dâ'â   food (i.e., cooking) fire

2. m bú' ta' tchû, 2·a m bú' ta'r dâ'â,

3. m bú' tchû, 3·a, m bú' dâ'â,

4. m ta'r tchû   4·a, on ta'r dâ'â

5. m 11 Hô tchû, 5·a, fire at which 'nanni & his brother cria

6·+ gau (:nanni's little haus)

7. Mé·ssiri Kâruma, My sister Kâruma (the corpse)

8. mouth of the grau

9. mound of earth and stones (the latter uppermost) 10. Fires

He said dead people become spirits and go into the moon, and you must pray to the beautiful moon for food and water because it is the home of the spirits. He called the orange-coloured halo around the moon *tkumin*, while we call it the corona.

!Nanni's father, /Umma-tchi-gua, taught him how to make a straw with which you could drink water from the crook of a tree, how to anticipate the rain by watching the movement of certain caterpillars, how to gather and prepare bush food and game, and how to build a hut from branches and grasses, and the boys built their own hut in the garden of Charlton House. Walking with Lucy and looking at the snapdragons, lupins and blowsy roses that had been taught to grow in this unfamiliar land, !Nanni paused in front of a flower that did not belong with all the others and said, *the white man's thing it is not, for a thing of the country it is.*

When I was in the Jagger Library at the University of Cape Town, I looked at some of Lucy's notebooks about the !Kun boys and I wrote down some of !Nanni's words that hold a trace of his voice and his story.

In my country when the sun has risen, the people sit by the fire to warm themselves. The people eat a fruit.

!Nanni does not eat the wild cat. I respect the wild cat.

I cry for my child. Somebody at sunrise killed my child.

The little elephant fell into the game pit. It did not die. Its mother took hold of it. Its mother pulled it out. It ran along. It did not die.

My father does not understand the white men. He sees the white men. He sees the Ovaherero. He has not seen the Namaque. Beating killed my father.

A little child has gone. They seek. They seek. They see him not.

!Nanni's country is far off.

He did not speak of how he was stolen from his home by the Makoba people or what happened to him during the months of his journey down to Walvis Bay on the Namibian coast, but it seems that his father was alive the last time he saw him. And then one morning at Charlton House he said to Lucy, 'I dreamt I saw my father. My father is dead.'

XXVI

11 September 2020. The side of a tooth broke off just after I got back from South Africa in March, but although my tongue kept relentlessly checking the rough edges, the tooth caused me no trouble and I have only just had it mended. The dentist was dressed in the full protective clothing that I have seen so often in newspaper photographs, her eyes hidden behind the glare of a plastic visor, her voice muffled but eager to be friendly.

Afterwards I walked through the marketplace where a few people were drifting around like nervous ghosts. I was told later that someone who had recently visited a cafe – I think it was called the Happy Goat but I might be wrong – had tested positive for corona, or perhaps had died of corona, I am not sure which. It reminded me of a traffic accident I witnessed years ago in London: a car standing at an odd angle on the pavement in front of the untidy heap of a body, and what I remember most vividly was the silence and the sense that time had slowed right down.

After the dentist I was lifting a guinea pig out of the run and I must have been very distracted because I managed to tangle one foot in the loose fence of chicken wire and I tumbled over and lay on the grass, the guinea pig cradled in my hand and a shooting pain in my ankle and me wondering what I would do if I could not stand up. But I could. I did. All was well.

Recently I have been emerging into a sort of half-state before the dawn in which I am neither awake nor asleep, and then it's as if I enter the periphery of a dream that belongs to someone else, and although I sense that things are happening there, I cannot quite see what those things are. I worry that I might be beginning to feel closer to the chickens, the sunlight on the quince tree, the humming of a bee, the scattering sound of a butterfly's wings on the windowpane than with the people who matter to me.

I have been trying to imagine the first two !Kun boys arriving at Cape Town harbour. I see them walking down the gangplank and entering the confusion of the streets. Some of the people who were involved in their capture and transportation referred to them as slaves, even though slavery had been abolished nearly fifty years earlier, and now I want to know if they were being held captive, with a rope perhaps, such as you might use for a stray dog, because otherwise they might run away.

Tamme and !Nanni had only met each other when they were about to be put on board the *Louis Alfred* in Walvis Bay and now they were being taken through the city to meet Lucy Lloyd. Maybe when they were handed over they trusted the gentleness of her manner. Maybe she had food to give them, to give them courage.

First to the museum with its hushed silences and its silent animals and then off to Mowbray. I am not sure how they would have got there. Was there a train? A carriage? I should try to find out in order to fill in the potholes in my mind which cause me to stumble.

They arrive at Charlton House and here comes /Han‡kass'o to welcome them, but he cannot speak or understand their language. Perhaps he shows them the kitten Kauki, the one who cannot hear. Do the children sleep in the same room where /Han‡kass'o sleeps? Does the kitten sleep with them?

I think Lucy spoke with the boys together, because that would make them less afraid. In the springtime of a September in South

Africa, it was probably often warm enough to sit outside in the garden, among the flowers. I also see them entering the dining room or Bleek's study for the first time; looking at the books, the paintings, the clock, the sewing machine and also at the Bushman artefacts: rattles made from the ears of springbok, shoes made from anteater skin, a decorated ostrich shell for carrying water.

In the first tentative exchanges that Lucy wrote down, the boys told her how to say, 'The cow eats, the dog barks, the cat eats the mouse, I blow out the lighted candle, I am sleepy . . . Jantje [/Han‡kass'o] takes Tamme to sleep.'

She learned that Tamme's people were the //Koo yau and their place was called Tsaba.

My mother's father was Little Tamme and my mother's mother was !Karo-//n'a. My father's father was Great Tamme.

He told her that *I ari* means 'to leave behind' and *//ku//kuno* means 'to picture for oneself distant things'.

From the notes I made during my one visit to the archive, I put together a few fragments of his story.

My father sewed a large bag. He put in the *//gue* fruit. My mother sewed the skin of the tou (a small antelope). My father had a wooden bow. My mother had a stick. She dug the ground.

My mother carried me on her back. The things I saw were numerous.

The Makoba got into their boat. I was here drinking water. The Makoba said 'Go into my house! There is plenty of food in my house!' I went into the Makoba house. My mother was seeking my mother's country's food. My mother entered the Makoba house. She gave the Makoba food . . . and on this day Tamme went away and this day the Makoba gave me to the Ovambo and the Ovambo gave Tamme to the White Man.

The Bushman women cry. The Bushman man is silent. The country's women have gone from this place. My one child has gone from this place.

The white man beats the horse . . . The people there were drunk.

The people have gone. I enter other people's uninhabited houses. I live in other people's uninhabited houses.

The place is black. We call it night. I call it night.

Along with what he said, Tamme made more than 140 drawings and paintings which gave form to 'what had been left behind or forgotten' – *I ari*; using *//ku//kuno*, 'to picture for oneself those distant things'.

Like !Nanni, he also made maps, but his maps included sketches of the people who lived in the different areas of the country. One of these sketches shows an Ovambo man with a child, ropes and a wooden boat, such as the one that first carried him away.

XXVII

16 September 2020. As I write this I am sitting by the sea. I listen to the soft rhythm of the waves. The sunshine is warm on one side of my face. I have just been swimming and the water was soupy grey but not cold and utterly calm, and for a while I stood at shoulder depth, the soft gravelly sand swallowing at my feet, planting me like a tree.

Where I started on the path that led to this particular stretch of coastline there was a notice saying that reptile specialists were collecting snakes, lizards and slow worms, newts, toads and frogs, in order to move them somewhere else, because this land of marsh and trees and tangled undergrowth, of blackberries ripening, birds tut-tutting and a peacock butterfly exhausted by the effort of summer, clapping its wings open to show with brightly painted eyes that it still lives – this land is scheduled to be torn apart by bulldozers so that a third nuclear power station can be built next to the first one which is not working but not decommissioned either, and a second one which does work but not very efficiently.

My heart sometimes races with the cacophony of the dangers that are crowding towards us from every direction. The loss of small things. The loss of enormous things. The sense of being voiceless in a world without pity. But I need to put all this to one side in order to see the !Kun boys as they try to navigate them-selves through their time.

The second two arrived six months later. They also had made a journey of several months from the place that was their home to Walvis Bay. /Uma was said to be in his teens, but he had the soft roundness of a young child, and Da was tiny and only six years old or maybe less. They were brought to Cape Town as part of what was called a 'consignment of Berg Damaras'.

I have just read that in 1878, Palgrave with his benign gaze and his bushy beard, along with the Cape governor, had annexed the port of Walvis Bay as a 'point of control' for trade and export. Palgrave had also drawn up the rules for what was called the Indentured Labour Scheme.

Between 1878 and 1882, hundreds of Damara families and many solitary children who were described as orphans were brought to Walvis Bay. The children had all been stolen and then sold and bartered in exchange for guns and now, on this the almost last leg of their journey, 'recruiters' were offered between five and ten shillings for each man, woman and child they could hand over, said to be 'willing to emigrate to the Cape Colony'.

These willing people were housed in a shed known as the Berg Damara Station until there were enough of them for a ship-ment. Before they left Namibia, an indenture form had to be signed on behalf of each individual, just to make sure that every-thing in the transaction was legal and above board.

I have been looking at one such form. It was drawn up in July 1880, on behalf of James Ayliff who was taking on a young child called Oura. With the flourish of his signature, Ayliff agrees to instruct Oura in the Christian Religion and the English Language and to provide him with Meat, Drink, Clothing and Lodging, along with a monthly wage. So far so good, but Oura is being represented by someone who is referred to as his Parent and the name of that someone, as it appears several times on the form, is 'Baboon'. Oh, how Mr Ayliff must have laughed at the joke.

Once the paperwork was complete and a big enough consignment had been collected in the Berg Damara Station, the people were put on trader Eriksson's ship – he of the three thousand tusks – the *Louis Alfred*, and they set off for Cape Town. Some of the indentured labourers had been ordered in advance: 'I have the honour to apply for a family of Damara servants as soon as a family will become available . . . it is desirable that the children be not more than two.' Others were sold again when they arrived at their final destination. /Uma and Da were brought to Lucy by Mr James Murray, the labour agent who had set up the shed in Walvis Bay.

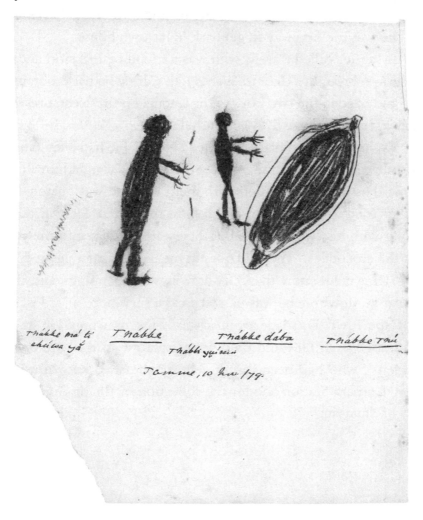

As with the other two boys, Lucy encouraged the children to make drawings and paintings, and bit by bit their stories also emerged. /Uma been taken by the Makoba along with his half-brother and they were brought 'to the Makoba's place'. Their father and the two mothers came to beg for their return, but they were threatened and could do nothing. They spent a last night near the camp and /Uma said that he watched the flames of the little fire they lit. His brother was not well and was returned to his family, but /Uma never saw his parents again.

He held up six fingers to show Lucy how many moons he had been with the Makoba. He said he was then given to a Boer in exchange for a gun. The Boer beat him and he managed to escape but he was too far away to get back to his own home.

A hunter called Carew, who was a friend of Eriksson and of Palgrave, brought /Uma to Walvis Bay. Carew had also obtained Da and handed the two boys to the traders on the coast, presumably in return for the five- or ten-shilling fee.

Da had lived in a place he called //Noma. He had been taught to hide when he saw strangers, but the Makoba caught him all the same. His mother wrestled with them and she was beaten. His father tried to shoot them and he was murdered. He was taken along with his two siblings, but they were thrown into the river for the crocodiles. 'They did not put me in the water,' he said.

/Uma made more than fifty drawings and paintings, and after a year at Mowbray he was passed on as a servant to a Mr Fischer of Cape Town. Da made around twenty-five drawings. He stayed on until March 1884 and then he was placed 'in the care of Mr Stevens', who had been responsible for the shed known as the Berg Damara Station and for the collection of the original delivery of children.

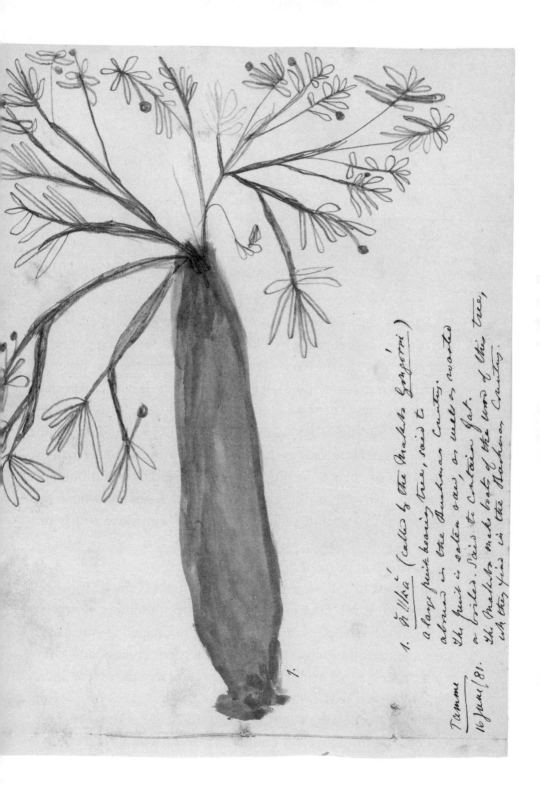

1. *Pillúa* (called by the Matebele Goaporré)

a large fruit bearing tree, said to
abound in the Bushman Country.

The fruit is eaten raw, as well as roasted
or boiled. Said to contain fat.
The Matebele make boats of the wood of this tree,
with they found in the Bushman Country.

Tammé
16 June/ 81.

XXVIII

13 October 2020. So much has happened and yet so little has happened. The days slipping by like the field mouse of the poem, or perhaps more like the harvest mice that I saw for the first time just recently, a number of them in glass containers as part of a project to try to return them to a cornfield where they could perhaps manage to survive. They were so tiny and intense, their eyes shining like black fires, their prehensile tails twirling like wire around a dry stalk of corn, tethering them if the wind blew, although no wind was blowing in the glass containers. A few days after the harvest mice, I set out on a six-and-a-half-hour drive south and west to a seaside town, with no stopping on the way, not even for a pee, which in retrospect was a bit odd.

I arrived in the afternoon. The town was crowded: people moving in slow, determined herds, their children scattering around them. People sitting down as if exhausted by the bright sunshine, smoking cigarettes, eating big ice creams and chips from paper boxes. Drinking whatever it was that they were drinking. Not much talk. Lots of boarded-up shops. Lots of dogs on leads and overflowing rubbish bins. Lots of densely tangled tattoos on bare arms and legs and shoulders. I felt as if I had entered a country I never knew existed, a country where I was a stranger who spoke a different language and followed different customs.

I was here to watch a play my son had been writing on and off for the last five years. It was being performed outdoors, the audience perched on concrete benches and facing a shallow marina, a little bridge on the far side of it, and out to sea beyond the bridge, the silhouette of an island called Steep Holm in English, Ynys Rhonech in Welsh.

The performance started at six, just as the early-evening sun was gathering up the energy of its departure. The sea was calm, seagulls dipping down into the glassy water. We were all given headphones to wear as we settled in our places like roosting birds. Music and my son's voice, his several voices, entered our consciousness through the strange intimacy of the headphones, while the silhouette of two figures walked and ran and held still in fixed positions on the bridge. I watched the sea, the reddening sun, the seagulls and the island, as if they were also part of the unfolding story.

I spent that night in a hotel. The hotel owner and his wife were both drunk in the evening and they were already getting drunk in the morning when I set off to my son's house in a nearby city to stay the following night with him and his wife and their two children. I walked into the kitchen and there they were: the children playing, a wood fire burning, the little garden held like a painting framed by the window.

And then I was on my way home, again driving without a break, and as I unlocked the door to my house I began to sob so loudly that the sound seemed to belong to a stranger, someone out of sight but standing close by.

I tried to be quiet. I tried to sleep. I tried to work on this book, but all the time I could feel the sensation of sobbing, and for a while it was as if the connection between me and my body and between my body and the world had been severed.

It passed. An orange bowl on the table is piled to the brim with quinces: their awkward naked shapes and their sweetly peculiar smell growing stronger as their skins turned more brightly yellow. The chickens and the guinea pigs need to be fed. Small spears of garlic are protruding from the earth in the vegetable bed. A soft rain is falling. *Opuopuonnu* is the /Xam word for a kind of rain that falls gently to the ground in little drops.

> *!khwa*: water, rain
> *kau*: to rain, to fall
> *!haken/haken*: a weak rain, mist
> *!kwobba*: fine rain
> */garaken-/garaka*: to make fine, be fine, fall gently
> */^ha*: rain, liquid
> *Obu:obu:ken*: to rain gently
> *opsoOpwonnu*: a weak rain

The virus that brought me home in March is again growing in strength. People struggling to breathe. People dying. People afraid of dying. My two children and their children were planning to come here over the holidays, but I do not know if they should dare to come, or if I should dare to let them come. Maybe we won't need to make a decision because some new law of disconnection will be passed, forbidding all movement.

I long with something like an ache in my bones for the gathered closeness of family. Without their physical presence I fear I might topple over in a strong wind like the harvest mice. I need to wrap my tail tightly around a dry stalk of corn.

Again I think of the /Xam and the !Kun children; all of them doing their best to hold tight in a world which has become utterly unfamiliar and more dangerous by far than the presence of a lion moving outside your sleeping place in the darkness of the night.

In a dream early this morning I found a photocopy of a picture of a group of people standing shoulder to shoulder. The image was blurred and I could not see their faces. I turned the picture over and on the blank page I wrote a letter to my husband. I told him he had been gone for such a long time and I would like him to come back.

All the Bushmen have left Charlton House. Now only Jemima and her four daughters, and her three sisters remain. They have very little money. In his will Bleek had requested that Lucy be paid something close to his own small salary by the library, so that she could continue with the work on the archive, but Lucy was a woman and she was not granted the status of her academic brother-in-law.

In 1879 David Livingstone's sister-in-law Elizabeth Lees Price came to visit the Lloyd sisters and described the encounter in her diary.

> These ladies are great students of Bushman and other African languages and habits . . . All (four) dressed in the same neat way, and the house was very very plain and simply furnished, with very little indeed in the way of ornament, a little too plain and bare I thought, but it was such a relief to feel in the company of people, refined, intellectual and cultivated, yet simple and homely as the humblest of cottagers.

In 1882 there was a conflict of interests between the trustees of the Grey Collection who supported Lucy and members of the South African Public Library committee who wanted to have her replaced by a man of their choosing. The case eventually went before the Cape Supreme Court, and when the verdict went against her, Lucy was 'relieved of her duties'. She was forty-seven years old and having never been physically strong she now felt so weak and demoralised that she said she hardly had the strength to write a letter.

She remained determined that 'the mass of material accumulated by Dr Bleek and myself', must be published and she finally achieved that aim two years before her death in 1914.

A precarious family clinging together and doing their best to survive. In 1884 Jemima and her daughters emigrated to

Germany where they could be helped by surviving members of Bleek's family in Bonn and in Berlin. Lucy held on, but in 1887 she and her older sister Fanny set sail for Europe, accompanied by a tin trunk which held at least 151 notebooks, the drawings by Dia!kwain and /Han‡kass'o and the four !Kun boys, as well as photographs of the informants who came to stay, and of other /Xam people, most of whom had been held in the Breakwater Jail. There was also a collection of copies of Bushman rock art that had been made by George Stow and which Lucy had bought for quite a bit of money, along with Bleek's intricate genealogical diagrams.

It seems that the two women stayed with their perfidious father's family in Wales for a while and they probably also went to England to stay with their maternal aunts and uncles. In 1889 Lucy and her two other sisters joined Jemima and her four daughters in Bonn, where they were staying with Bleek's relatives. In spite of being exhausted and unwell, Lucy continued with her work on the /Xam interviews. She indicated that 'about 4534 half-pages or columns (in 54 volumes quarto)' had been collected after Bleek's withdrawal from the project in May 1875. Of these 'only about 1,776 had been translated into English', leaving some 3,000 untranslated pages still to be done. In 1896 Swan Sonnenschein of London offered to publish her *Specimens of Bushman Folklore*, but because Lucy insisted on keeping the phonetic /Xam text next to her translations the project was eventually abandoned.

By 1898 Lucy and Fanny, along with the metal trunk, had moved to Berlin, probably to a flat in the Charlottenburg district. This was her home address when she wrote to her friend George McCall Theal in 1904 asking if he could in any way help with the publication of her book. He was by now a prolific and popular writer on South African history and so he was able to use his influence to persuade George Allen & Co. of London to publish Lucy's life's work.

On 8 December 1908, the first batch of sixteen pages of proofs were sent to her in Charlottenburg and the final batch arrived two years later, almost to the day. Lucy had completed a draft preface in May 1911, but her words were much edited by McCall Theal. He oversaw the entire project and provided an extraordinary introduction in which he declared: 'there is no longer room on the globe for palaeolithic man . . . progress is remorseless . . . and the pygmy hunter with his bow and poisoned arrows could not be permitted to block the way.'

In this same introduction Lucy's 'givers of native History' are transformed into ' "savages" whose minds were like those of little children in all matters not connected with their immediate bodily wants', while she herself, after almost forty years of solitary work on the project, is described as being Bleek's 'editor and assistant'. She is complimented for her 'boundless patience, untiring zeal and an acute ear', but the name of the great man himself, 'should be uttered not only with the deepest respect, but with a feeling akin to reverence.'

And now I have a memory which suddenly comes back and shocks me with its presence. In 1978 when the page proofs of my book *The White Men* were ready to be checked, I had just given birth to my first child, and because there was a need to hurry, my editor turned up at the Guy's Hospital Maternity Ward and we went through the text with the curtains closed around the bed in which I lay, my little daughter at my breast.

With a strange echo of Lucy's experience, I had been told a few months previously that publication could only go ahead if I agreed to the inclusion of a foreword written by a much-respected American professor of anthropology. My Dutch friend Sandra was staying with me and my husband in the huge and dusty warehouse that was our home when the foreword arrived and she says I wept like a child as I read it. The professor described my book as 'educational and entertaining' and, in complete contradiction to everything I had been thinking and writing about, he confidently declared 'all who met a white man could not help admiring him and subjecting themselves entirely to his will.'

Specimens of Bushman Folklore was published in 1912. It did not create much of a stir, but thanks to the authority of McCall Theal's name it was at least taken seriously. In that same year, Lucy and Fanny, along with the metal trunk, arrived in Cape Town and move into Charlton House, where Jemima's three surviving daughters were still living.

In 1913 Lucy Lloyd was awarded an honorary doctorate by the University of Cape Town, and there is a photograph of her dressed in the black robes and mortar board of her new condition, holding the rolled-up proof of her achievement in her left hand. The expression on her face appears hopeful, fearful and determined as

she gazes out into some faraway distance that she seems to be on the edge of entering. When she died a year later there were still thousands of words waiting to be translated out of her phonetic /Xam into her careful and slightly archaic English.

Jemima's daughter Dorothea carried on with the work. She gave much of the archive to the University of Cape Town, but always kept the notebooks with her and people remembered seeing them on the bookshelves just above the writing desk in her study. It was only with her death in 1947 that the notebooks finally went to join their companions as part of the Bleek Collection in what was called the Bleek Seminar Room and no mention of Lucy Lloyd anywhere to be seen.

In 1962, a scholar called Otto Spohr heard of their existence but did not consult them. In 1973, Roger Hewitt, a student of anthropology at London University, wished to consult them in the flesh as it were, but was told they had vanished. He offered an hourly rate to whoever would search for them and three weeks later the notebooks were found languishing in some dark cupboard or on some dusty shelf in the Extension Building at the back of the university's Jameson Hall. Hewitt produced his doctoral study of the Bleek–Lloyd notebooks in 1976.

XXIX

25 October 2020 and the rain is soft and very cold. My new but very old cockerel died a week ago and I miss his gentlemanliness. On his last day he found a slug and danced around the garden holding it in his beak while making vague noises of triumph, but the burst of energy did not last long and he went to sit beside the entrance to the chicken house, slumped and exhausted, his three wives keeping close. That night he shuffled off his little life and in the morning I buried him. I put a few marigold flowers on his bright orange feathers, before covering him over and planting a lily on top. My neighbour who always has a surfeit of bantams has given me a young cockerel who is nice enough, but nothing like so courteous, although he does carry a wonderful mix of colours: an oily body shimmer of blue, black and green and a golden ruff around his neck.

> A person who dies, the rain falls, taking away his footsteps, so that his footsteps may no longer be seen. Therefore, when we are putting him in the grave, just as we are filling in the earth, the rain falls before we have covered him over. Finished, our thoughts rise up, leaving us, while our bodies are those which lie in the earth. Therefore our thoughts leave us. (‡Kasin)

My husband's birthday, which was also his death day seven years ago, has been and gone. My son and his family did not come for the ritual of that remembrance because there was Covid in the schools of both their children. My granddaughter did not stay with me because of Covid, although she and my daughter and my daughter's husband will again come and spend a few days in a campsite close to the sea and I'll visit them there, in spite of Covid.

We are few. It was so.

I dreamt of fish swimming in a stone trough and the water was draining out of it. I dreamt I met an old lover who in life has become a very old man. In the dream he was as young as he once was, sitting at the far end of a long table, but he could not hear me when I tried to speak to him.

The two short weeks I spent in South Africa are vivid in my mind, as if lit by that brightening of the sky which comes just before a storm breaks; a crowd of images to be pulled out like a thread of silk from a cocoon that has been plunged in hot water; each day ready to unspool itself.

Conversations, faces, rooms, beds, landscapes and streets. Here I am in a library turning over the pages in one of Lucy's notebooks; in a market trying to decide which little painting to buy for a sum of money that would also get me a cup of coffee; picking up the skull of what I think must have been a meerkat lying on the gravelly ground; watching as panicky and bedraggled sheep are being herded into a compound by men on motorbikes.

I had expected to be gone for at least a month, and if I had learned of the fast spread of Covid one day later, I suppose I might still be staying with Tim and Claire and young Adam: an accidental guest in a wooden house a few minutes' walk from a beach that looks out towards the Antarctic. As it was I got back just in time, the battered mother-of-pearl helmet of the abalone shell that I found on the beach safely wrapped among my jumpers and socks.

I notice it every day. It shimmers on the wall like the exhalation of a dream, providing me with the tangible proof that not so long ago I was somewhere else.

When preparing for the trip to South Africa I bought a travel guide that was ten years out of date, but I never thought to look at it. I spoke to a friend who said he would like to come with me and he said we could hire a very modern truck with a tent that sprang open on its roof, to keep us safe from lions when we were sleeping in the red desert. It was only then I realised he was meaning to go to north-east Namibia, while I was meaning to go to a part of the Karoo where there are no lions.

I have a limited sense of geography and I hardly glanced at the map of the Northern Cape that someone gave me, showing the orientation of place, the length of distance. Years ago, when I went to the island of St Helena in the South Atlantic, I kept thinking I was going to Elba in the Mediterranean, and even after I knew that was not the case, I allowed the mistake to linger. And when I went to Mauritius in search of stories about my father's complex ancestry of race and paranoia, the island was so different to what I had expected, so overwhelmed by the demands of tourism, that I went to stay on the adjacent island of Rodrigues instead: a flat and almost barren land inhabited by the descendants of runaway slaves, and in the encounters I had there I felt a sense of some sort of homecoming, even though I could claim no roots of belonging.

Before setting off I packed a small suitcase with just enough room for the walking boots which I abandoned when I left so the abalone shell could take their place. Three pairs of socks, lots of knickers, thin pale trousers that looked as if they were expecting me to be keen on playing golf, and two equally pale and vaguely luminous T-shirts designed to reflect the sunlight and make me less hot when under its glare. Herbal sleeping pills that don't do much, but I like the cow's-breath taste of them, strong insect repellent that caught at the back of my throat whenever I used it, sandals, a bright-coloured skirt, an old pair of black cotton trousers which were a bit tight, a shirt, a blouse, three propelling pencils, six soft-covered notebooks and one big hard-backed notebook.

I had liked the sound of the word Karoo from the moment I first heard it. I looked at a few photographs and from them I began to anticipate the landscape, and because I read somewhere that the sandy desert is sprinkled with tiny rubies, I could see them glistening like drops of blood. I placed everything under the hard monotheistic stare of the sun by day, the soft and more forgiving gaze of the moon by night.

> We do not feel nice when the sky is black. The path would be white for us if the place were shining from the moon. When we are going home in the moon's light, we see our footprints as we return. (Dia!kwain)

I listened to the cry of unfamiliar birds.

> The little bird /ka Kau is not eaten by the Bushmen. It lives in trees and flies about. It says tcha tcha tcha when it is laughing at the wild cat. The other birds hearing it laughing, go to it. They all laugh at the wild cat. (Tamme)

Springbok moved close enough for me to see the stripes on their faces, and I watched as kudu, eland, gemsbok and ostrich moved purposefully forward, and saw the footprints of the beautiful cat-like creature called the caracal, the swooping trail of a snake, the burrow of a porcupine. And the odd thing is that now, even though I have been and come back and nothing was as I thought it might be, the perfect world I had imagined remains nestled in my mind, waiting to be hatched into some other reality.

XXX

29 October 2020. I visited my friend John this afternoon; he who was going to come with me to South Africa, until we realised that our plans were not the same. John lives nearby with his husband Rob who is an opera singer. They have twelve orange-coloured goats smelling of goat and four dogs smelling of dog and a Hermann's tortoise who sits under a reading lamp in the kitchen and sometimes sits close to a dog, craning its neck to stare eye to eye, doing its best to be friendly in a reptilian sort of way.

They also have peacocks, and I watched the male performing the final stage of seducing one of his wives. He turned the full spread of his burlesque fan into a sort of tent around his head and rattled the feathers, the sound so loud and fierce I could hear arrows falling at the Battle of Agincourt. It made me think of the courtship dances of the ostrich and then the ostrich dance of the /Xam.

> The men call like the male ostrich; the women clap their hands for them; the men call like the male ostrich to the women. They call excellently, for their throat sounds like a real ostrich; while the women are those who sing. While the women are those who dance. (/Han‡kass'o)

John said we are all suffering from present-traumatic stress, as the exploding bomb of this pandemic keeps hitting us suddenly and unexpectedly. And then the shock passes and we potter on, like the peacocks potter on, like the guinea pigs and chickens potter on. Long ago I was in Portugal with my first husband, waiting at a bus station, and pigeons were pecking at the tarmac where some corn had been spilt. A bus arrived and the pigeons flew up with a clatter of wings, but one of them was too slow and was squashed. Within seconds the others returned to finish the corn around the blood and feathers of their companion.

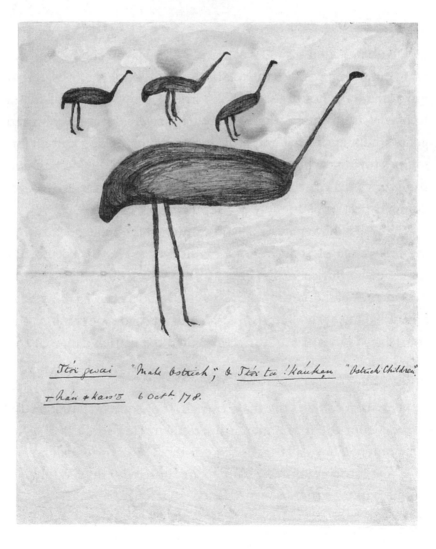

I still often comfort myself with the lines from a poem by Valéry, 'Le vent se lève. Il faut tenter de vivre.' Sometimes I lie in bed and sing it in English and my voice that was never very tuneful emerges as an odd growl. The wind rises. We must attempt to live.

I have become a bit of a coward. I am afraid of watching films that might turn violent, I am even afraid of radio plays with a sinister psychological edge to them. I listen to old reruns of Sherlock Holmes or Hercule Poirot in which they gently unravel illogical murders, or I watch Inspector Montalbano solving crimes in Sicily, his face reminding me of an old friend who lives in Berlin and who I would like to visit if visiting was something that could be done. Anyway, there is the inspector in an elegant and decaying seaside town, confronting the dead bodies of pretty young women, and villainous old and young men, and because everything is resolved in the end I am able to fall into an easy sleep. I wake convinced I have dreamt of nothing until the wispy recollection of a dream jumps out and startles me.

I dreamt of my father. My father is dead.
And Mother asked me, did I not see that the dream I had dreamt had spoken the truth? We now saw what had made me dream it.

I have been trawling through a file I put together a couple of years ago, filled with photocopied pages from books that I thought might help me with this book. According to one floating page, 210,000 upright pianos were made in the United States in 1882, and 120,000 elephants were killed in that same year. Meanwhile the US election is getting closer, the choice between the red and the blue, Trump or Biden.

Once I got to South Africa I was surrounded by so many images of destruction. I knew about the destruction of the /Xam whose way of thinking seems to have taken up residence inside my head, but nothing had prepared me for the destruction of the animals and the landscape that held them. And then my journey was cut short, leaving me suspended between what was and what might have been.

n-uz: to disappear
turruwa: to forget the past

When I was making a few vague plans for my journey, a friend told me I just had to rent a truck in Cape Town and drive to a town called Calvinia. A straight and tarmacked road and one day should do it. The Karoo is the safest place in all the world, he said, and I saw myself sitting boldly at the wheel, foot pressed down on the accelerator.

XXXI

3 November 2020. We are approaching a second lockdown, but it has none of the sense of purpose that belonged to the first. Then there was an end in sight, now there is only a mist creeping up from all sides.

> Therefore father told me that at the time war intended to come to us, our mist sat there. The people fought us in the mist. And at the time when the people had finished fighting with us and they went away leaving us, the mist also went away, leaving us. (Dia!kwain)

But this now is the start of my recollection of the two weeks I spent in South Africa from 5 to 20 March 2020. There I was in that more innocent time, arriving at an unknown airport, blinking in the daylight, pulling a shiny black suitcase on its wheels, and there was Tanya, in whose house I was going to stay, waiting for me.

She wore a bright flowery dress and she was carrying a bunch of the South African giant protea flowers that resemble artichokes, but with a tinge of pink, and she was waving them at me like a welcoming flag. I was exchanging spring for autumn and had already removed my thick tights and my coat in the ladies' loo and stuffed them into the suitcase. Tanya could not remember where she had parked her car and so we spent a while looking for it in an underground car park that looked like all other underground car parks and eventually we found it and sped off towards the city. She honked her horn a lot and muttered or shouted imprecations at other drivers and I felt as if we had been friends for ages. We reached a high locked gate that pulled itself open with a command from her ignition key and then closed itself and locked us into safety.

I stepped out into a little garden crowded with beehives and stacks of wooden trays for the honeycomb and lots of other bits and pieces waiting to be used for something. Two plump clumber spaniels came to welcome their mistress and wriggled their bottoms at me while remaining aloof. I was introduced to John, who worked in the house and who looked like a schoolmaster, and to Sarah, who was young and thin and pregnant. There was an almost silent man who spent most of his time working outside, helping with the beehives I think.

A house of books and paintings and shuttered windows. The absent-presence of Tanya's husband Heinz who had died a few months before, and she was missing him with that first sharp pain when it seems as if the person who has abandoned life is bound to walk back through the front door, to explain that it has all been a foolish mistake. I was shown my room with a single bed, a table and a chair, and a little bathroom leading from it. The flowers were put in a vase and there was a packet of raisins and a bottle of water and other small details of welcome. For many years Tanya had been head of the Special Collections Department at the University of Cape Town, and she had put together a selection of books and articles relating to the /Xam which she thought might be relevant. I felt like a student newly arrived at university.

I also felt unutterably weary. The weariness of being welcomed as a stranger. The weariness of concentration. The weariness of not quite knowing what I was doing here, what I was expecting to find. I was introduced to Tanya's son and to her pregnant daughter-in-law who lived in part of the house. John and Sarah waited to be told what to do next. The dogs padded about.

Tanya had a hectic and amiable energy; it was as if she was always ready to go into hiding at a moment's notice. Her parents were members of the ANC, and in the 1960s when she was a teenager, they were banned and escaped to Zambia, while she stayed on in South Africa. A few years later she was also banned and so she joined them until the apartheid era was brought to an end.

Thanks to my habit of never putting a date to anything and jumping from one notebook to the next, I am not sure of the sequence of the days, but I think it was on the following morning that I went to the Company's Gardens. Not that it matters.

I see myself sitting outside an elegant cafe, drinking a glass of fruit juice that had been served with a lot of flourish. Black waiters to serve the white guests who all seemed to have a look of entitlement that I had not expected. Pigeons milling about as pigeons do, making an everywhere out of anywhere. An Afrikaans woman came over to my table and handed me a white napkin, saying, 'Wave it! It frightens them!' At first I did not understand who she was referring to, until I realised it was the pigeons. I had scattered some biscuit crumbs for them, so her solicitousness was also a criticism.

I left the cafe and walked past the dark bronze statue of Cecil Rhodes giving what appeared to be a Nazi salute. A woman with a battered face came up to me and said she was looking for a talk, which I presumed was something to do with religion, and so I said, 'No thank you.' A man with red hair asked, 'How are you today?' offering me a Love Project Card, which also seemed to have a religious implication, and with the same formal English politeness, I said, 'Fine, thank you,' and he left me alone.

A belligerent cannon was commemorating the triumph of some nineteenth-century battle and beyond it the old Slave Lodge had been transformed into the Museum of Art. A group of men were sleeping face down on the closely mown grass, and at some sign I did not see, they all got to their feet and drifted off. Maybe they had been warned that the police were approaching. I thought of a line from an Argentinian song written at the time of the Disappearances, 'Quick, my darling, call the robbers, the police are coming.'

I found the Museum of Natural History and walked up its broad stone steps, that would not have been out of place in how I imagine America's Deep South. I remember the shock of the change that came from stepping out of the sunshine and into the cool interior. I bought a ticket – I must have bought a ticket – from three young people in uniform behind a desk, or perhaps they were four of them, or two. And then I set off to explore the rooms. There were no other visitors, just a few guards, who stood as silent and motionless as the exhibits.

I was startled by the sheer size of the glass cabinets. The creases on the body of the lion were like the weathering of wind and sand on his skin, giving a sense of the fluidity and power of movement. The hanging dewlaps on an eland as big as a cow appeared like part of a ceremonial costume, and its honey-coloured skin was also decorated with intimate creases and wrinkles at the neck, the leg and the chest. A group of springbok were caught by the taxidermist in the act of running and leaping and one of them had its face turned towards me.

When we see an antelope near our other person's place, that place where our person has died, we respect the antelope, for the antelope's legs seem small, it is our person who has died. It is a spirit antelope. (!Nanni)

The snarl on the face of the jackal exposed the bright pinkness of painted gums.

The jackal head hair is red, her ears being red, her back being black, her nose being long, her face being pointed, for her ears are pointed. So she must marry a jackal for they all have ears that are pointed. Their backs are black. Their bodies are red. Their legs are red. They scream as they walk. (/A!kunta)

I paused in front of an aardwolf and remembered seeing one in the Amsterdam Zoo tiptoeing on stilt-like legs, painfully timid in spite of its fierce appearance. They live on insects, and even then, some forty years ago, the species was on the edge of extinction.

The aardwolf marries a she aardwolf who lives in a cave. He feels he always wants to live in a cave when he was a man. He is a man, he is an aardwolf. He speaks. He lives in a cave with aardwolf children because they always used to be in a cave when they were people who talked. (//Kabbo)

Each creature inhabited its own logical perfection of form. Their stillness made me think of the Chinese terracotta army that waits for the order to return to battle. A Cape fox was surrounded by the busy life of babies that would never grow old. A pangolin was weighed down by the defensive but useless armour of geometric scales. One cabinet held a nest of sociable weavers; the little birds flitting silently and without motion, in and out of the protective bulk of their home that was as big as the body of an elephant. Wherever I walked through the rooms of this necropolis, I was accompanied by recordings of whales singing. At one point I stopped in front of a closed door, and through a side window I could see all sorts of antelopes encased in sheets of bubble wrap.

I passed an asteroid with an explanation that it had been brought into being when the solar system was formed. It was made mostly from iron and nickel and weighed 750 kilos, and the one that caused the extinction of the dinosaurs would have been composed of similar material but was much larger.

I spoke with a guard for the sake of speaking and tried to ask him about the whereabouts of the Bushmen exhibits, but I was vague in my questioning and he was vague in his answer. When I had completed my tour of the museum and was back at the desk, I asked the question more clearly and I was told that the exhibits had been moved but no one quite knew where to.

I was referring to a collection of plaster casts of groups of Bushmen that I had seen in photographs. They had been there to welcome visitors in the entrance hall. Groups of people in their own glass cases, being themselves, just as the Cape fox and the springbok were also there and being themselves. I think they were /Xam and I know that the men were cast from the prisoners in the Breakwater Jail, while the women must have been domestic servants. They were portrayed as family groups, but there were no children included, presumably because children could not be forced to keep still, no matter how severely they were ordered to do so. In one display the Bushmen were shown in their little huts of branch and grass, busy with the work of grinding seeds on a grinding stone, decorating ostrich eggs, stitching skins, cutting flints for spearheads.

> The Bushmen, when without a knife, use a stone knife for cutting up game. They break a stone, knocking off a flat splinter from it and cut up the game with that. The Grass Bushmen make arrow heads of white quartz crystal points. (//Kabbo)

In another glass case, they were gathered in an approximation of the desert at night and they were dancing to silent music and song around the plaster flames of a campfire.

The drum which the women beat sounds well. Therefore the men dance well, because the drum which the women beat sounds well. The dancing rattles which the men tie to their feet sound well. (/Han‡kass'o)

In the photographs the people appear as vivid as all the other creatures that are on show, caught in a moment of activity, just as the springbok and the sociable weavers were caught. But for all the accuracy of the execution of form, skin colour and hair, bracelet and cloak, for all the elegance of their poised movement and the concentration with what they were seeming to do, nothing could hide the tragic solemnity of their facial expression, that same sad and distant gaze which characterises //Kabbo and his companions.

The Bushmen displays were made from life; the naked bodies of the subjects turned into plaster casts. Such a process is a disconcerting and uncomfortable experience to go through, and a cast of a face is an especially difficult thing to endure. The subject must keep still, eyes closed, a straw in each nostril to breathe through; the trapped sensation of wet plaster gripping on the skin as it dries and warms and turns hard.

Apart from the complete bodies and faces of the people, the museum curators also wanted a detailed record of the sexual parts of the Bushmen, both the men and the women, so an extensive collection was made of this one area of anatomy. Wet plaster drying on the hips and pelvis, on the penis and testicles, on the vagina, labia and buttocks. Once it had set, the mould was cut and prised off and taken away to be reassembled; the finished products kept in an upstairs room, to be viewed in the name of science, or in the name of prurient fascination. They must also still be somewhere, but I did not ask. I also did not ask about the collection of Bushman skulls and skeletons. Many years ago, a friend who did some of the photography for my book *The*

White Men was in the Antwerp Anthropological Museum in Belgium, and as an unexpected and somehow special favour, the curator invited him into a private room where they kept a complete male Bushman as a taxidermy specimen, like a fairground monster.

XXXII

5 November 2020. Joe Biden is almost winning the race for the White House and Donald Trump is playing golf. Yesterday morning I made some grapefruit marmalade and put the last scrapings from the pan into a little dish. In the afternoon I gave a friend a piece of toast spread with some of the marmalade taken from the dish. During the night I got into a panic because I thought I might have tasted a spoonful of the marmalade and then used that spoon without washing it and perhaps I was carrying the virus asymptomatically, in which case I had fatally poisoned my friend.

> The people who die of sorcery are not yet sufficiently strong . . . the sorcerers are not people who are ordinary Bushmen and when these sorcerers bewitch us, we die without feeling ill. (Dia!kwain)

There was nothing outwardly wrong with me. I had none of the signs that are supposed to denote the presence of Covid in the body: no cough, no fever, no lack of taste of salt or sweet, just the overriding sense of not being real, like a ghost of myself. I licked the palm of my hand in the dark of the night, to check that I existed.

The seed of my fear must have sprouted a few days before the lockdown, when I hugged my daughter and I was hugged by my granddaughter around my knees and I stroked her hair and I was hugged by one friend and then by another – always the sideways embrace with the face averted and always with people who had been careful to keep themselves protected, so it should have been OK. But now I could see the dancing spheres of the virus, jumping like fleas from one human body to the next.

I suppose we are all carrying a complicated sense of responsibility for what is happening. We have caused such damage to the world in which we live, and we know that even when the first force of this pandemic has passed, there is bound to be more trouble to follow.

In order to escape such thoughts, I need to follow the path of my time in the Cape. Again I am not sure if the sequence is right, but at some point in those first days, I went to stay for two nights with Tim and Claire and Adam. Tim collected me and we drove past the townships, with the occasional glimpse of the elegant homes of the people who did not live in the townships. We saw several sacred ibis which were much loved by the ancient Egyptians, but here they go by the name of bin chicken because they feed themselves by dipping their beautiful heads into rubbish bins. We reached another garage gate that opened with a secret command from the safety of the car and there were warning notices on the fences surrounding the quiet little house in this sleepy village, just as on the fences surrounding any house that was worth defending from intruders.

That afternoon Tim and I walked to the sea. A bay of white sand and dark rocks and the shock of seeing people in a place where any human activity felt like an intrusion. Some thirty figures in wetsuits were bobbing in the water trying to catch the waves with their surfboards, and I kept replacing them with a family of sea otters bobbing among the kelp. A fur seal instead of a swimmer, Cape penguins instead of dogs on leads. The bin chicken reinstated as the sacred ibis. I added a band of Khoekhoen who once lived by this shore and were known as strand loopers or beach walkers. They could have a camp under the dense canopy of milkwood trees. Their shell middens could replace the overflowing rubbish bins.

We returned to the smiling presence of young Adam and the smiling welcome of Claire who has none of my vague fear but regularly sets off on her own in a truck, driving for hundreds of miles to Zambia or Mozambique or Botswana; expeditions lasting several weeks as she pursues her studies of the honeyguide birds which lead people to the nests of wild bees. The bartering of larvae in exchange for honey.

I often wonder how we would have managed if I had been their guest for several months. I would have grown familiar with the coastline, the tortoises, the moods of the weather, the fierceness of the ocean, and I am sure I would have learned to love the plump contentment of Adam, watching over him like an unexpected aunt as he grew and began to make words and to rise up onto his feet.

I liked the garden. It was not much more than a scattering of stones on hard soil with bushes called cancer bushes growing wild and a few other plants that had been persuaded to grow in the face of the wind and the sun. The stones lay about like old bones or wind-dried corpses, and a particularly long and lumpy one had the size of a man and the shape of a lizard.

The next day Tim and I and young Adam set off for an area known as Olifantsbos in the Cape Point Reserve. The reserve's high metal fence was close to their house, but to get to the entrance we had to drive some way. We paid a fee at the main gate and suddenly there were animals to be seen: bonteboks with their mask-like faces, their sharp straight horns, and I could understand the tapping sensation in which you feel the weight of horns on your head, the black stripes decorating your face, and the dried vegetation that rustles as you pass through it on small, sharp hoofs. A group of springbok, ten or twelve of them perhaps, were held together as if they were a single body and I tried to multiply them into a vast living river twenty miles wide and fifty miles long.

We reached the coast. A quiet cluster of bonteboks watched us from the far end of the bay. The white boulders looked like sheep, but no sheep were here, and thanks to their absence I could get a sense of the wildness and profusion of what once had been. Ostriches were undulating across the land like ships in full sail, so different from the bedraggled groups of domesticated ostrich behind fences that we had passed on the road.

> Up to 1860 it was commonly thought that the day was not far distant when the ostrich would be numbered amongst the extinct animals of the world. As the process of extermination went on, the wild birds were scared away from their old haunts . . . but a new industry was to be added to our domesticated list with an industry that would cause large tracts of country to be fenced in . . . by strong wire fences five feet high and subdivided into numerous camps with similar fences . . . By 1882 253,954 pounds of ostrich feathers for export were valued at the Cape Custom House at £1,093,989. (George McCall Theal, 1889–1900)

> The Ostrich walks out of the water, it basks in the sun at the water's edge, because it is still a young Ostrich. Its feathers are young feathers (quills) because its feathers are little feathers. They are black, for a little male Ostrich he is . . . He eats young bushes because a young Ostrich he is. He swallows young plants which are small, because a little Ostrich he is. (/A!kunta)

Sun and wind. White sand littered with huge strips of dry kelp and branches of whitened wood and shells and stones. I could be happy here for months, I thought, staring down, staring out, picking something up and letting it drop. Picking something up and keeping it for the sake of the hieroglyphs of memory that I could bring back with me when I eventually returned home.

We began to walk in the direction of the southernmost tip of Africa. I watched the silhouette of black rocks scattered into the ocean and, drawing closer, I realised two fur seals were part of the silhouette, both of them absolutely still in the sunshine, their heads pointed upwards towards the sky. And all the while the rubbery strips of the kelp kept turning and stirring on the surface of the water like crowds of marine beasts at play. There might have been a sea otter or two, but we had no binoculars with which to bring them into focus. Tim said that poachers come at night to dive for abalone shells among the great forests of kelp and cut at the roots of these strange underwater trees that can be several hundred years old.

I was in Gibraltar not so long ago, visiting a vast cave that was one of many dwelling sites used by the Neanderthals, a Neanderthal city it has been called, although most of the caves and the evidence that they held and still hold, have been swallowed by the sea. The people lived on limpets and other small bits of life, their teeth worn almost flat from the sand that got into everything. They remained there for tens of thousands of years, while here we are, only a tiny step from our beginnings and already approaching what feels like the end of our tenancy.

Adam has his face against Tim's chest. The wind blows fine sand at us. The sun is sharp but somehow sweet. I find my abalone shell sunk into the sand. It has been mined by worms so that no poacher would want it anyway, but the worms have given it an intricate surface as beautiful as fine lacework.

We stop beside the skeleton of what is left of a whale next to the skeleton of what is left of an iron ship. The black and the white. The old and the new.

And then when we have gone far enough, we turn to go back. We come to a choice between a higher path and a lower path

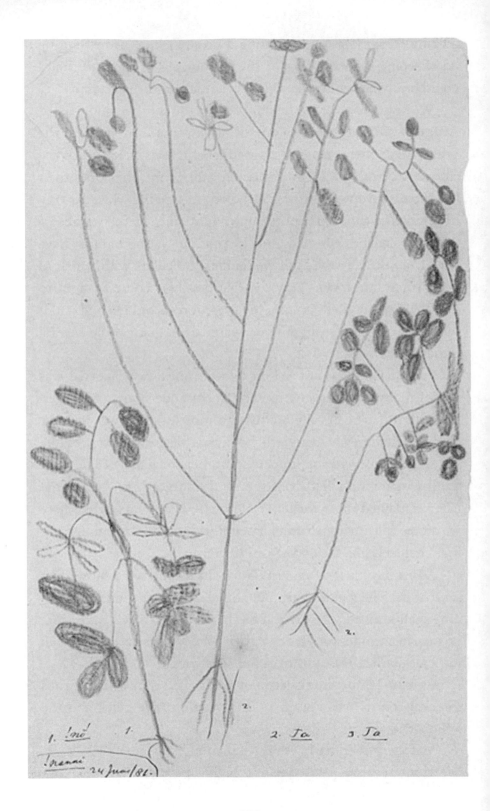

1. *Inó*   1.

Inanai 24 Juni/81.

2. *Ta*   3. *Ta*

which stays closer to the ocean. Tim sets off on the higher one and I keep low. There is a steep bank on my right, thick with bushes, and a baboon is sitting on its haunches, staring at me.

I keep walking and the baboon slowly makes his way to the edge of the path and waits for me. He faces me, redolent with authority. I look away as if I am shy which perhaps I am and I walk resolutely on, which I was told later was the right thing to do. The baboon allows me to pass, and once I have done so, he clambers back up the bank and returns to his sentinel duties.

> Dia!kwain heard from his mother that the baboons were formerly people, at that time at which we who are people, were not here.

Dia!kwain also told how the baboons used to come to listen, when the instrument known as the ‡gebbi-gu was being played, and as the women sang, the baboons would join in with the singing.

> The baboons sing, making a sound like the Bushmen women.
>
> They come to watch the Bushmen holding the ‡gebbi-gu. They listen to the ‡gebbi-gu tune which the women sing. They also sing the tune which the Bushmen women sing.
>
> One baboon sings before the other baboons, for he wants them to sing after him, that they may sing the ‡gebbi-gu as he does. For Bushmen also do this. One woman stands and sings first and she sings to the others as she wants them to sing after her.

XXXIII

10 November 2020. Boris Johnson says he's as fit as a butcher's dog. I imagine an old-fashioned butcher's shop, sawdust on the floor, rabbits and pheasants hanging by their feet from hooks. The butcher's dog grabs a string of sausages and runs out into the street. The butcher gives chase. I think he throws a meat cleaver at the dog. The cleaver misses the dog. The dog swallows the sausages.

The sun has returned. It shines bright and clear into the studio where I am sitting. Silence, apart from the soft thud of my fingers on the laptop. I wish I had learned to touch-type. I once did a course called Sight and Sound and that should have done the trick, but I cheated by looking down at the keys when we were told to keep our eyes closed.

In a little while I will go out and walk through the woods that lead to a stretch of the sea, via the sudden beauty of reed beds. I enjoy the familiarity of the repetition of a path that I have walked so many times.

While I was with Tim and his family I arranged a meeting with Kerry Jones. She is a linguistic anthropologist and she works with different Bushman groups in Upington and over to the north-east of the Kalahari with the N'uu, the !Kun, the Khue of Platfontein, and the Ju/'hoansi of Namibia. When she is not with them, she lives in the next village along the coast from Scarborough and her partner is a professional surfer.

My first impression was of a quite formal young blonde woman, but once we had started talking I realised I was the cause of the formality. She questioned me about what I was doing here, why I was thinking that I could write something new about the /Xam and what I wanted from my trip. I tried to explain myself as well as I could and she seemed to accept my explanation. She said that if I wanted to get anywhere then I had to be real with the people I saw, because they would not accept any sort of pretence. 'You have to trust yourself as a person and they will learn who you are from watching you and in that way they will know if you are authentic or not.'

She said that all the Bushmen she worked with hated being viewed as subjects for academic study. Scientists would turn up in their jeeps and without so much as a by your leave they wanted to collect mouth swabs that would allow a genetic sequencing to be analysed. Earnest anthropologists arrived with tape recorders, demanding authentic ancestral stories, unsullied by the facts of the harsh present world in which the people were now living. No jokes or modern references, just a pure mythic time in which the Wind's son who was formally a man became a bird who lived in the mountain; of the girl of the Early Race who made the stars; of the origin of death. Lots of sorcerers and trances and incantations and no mention of the Boers or the prisons, the indentured labour, the theft of children, the loss of language and of the land which the language had once defined and claimed as its own.

Kerry told me of an anthropologist getting excited about the golden waters of the Karoo, which he thought was to do with the world's first beginnings, although what was really being spoken about was a powerful golden liquid called whisky.

She told me a story of the origin of the naming of a salt pan known as Moravet. A long time ago, a good rain fell and there were lots of insects, and the bat-eared foxes ate so many of them, they became fat. The people caught the bat-eared foxes and cooked them and skimmed off the fat, which they poured into a huge container, and they ate so much of it that they fell asleep. When they woke and saw the container, they greeted it as if it were another person, '*Môre vet!*', which is a Bushman Afrikaans way of saying, 'Good day to you, fat!' And that is how one particular salt pan with a glistening white surface earned its name. She said I must visit a salt pan in the evening when there is a full moon, so that I can see the beauty of it and the way the salt crystals and the moon answer each other, light for light.

I thought of Dia!kwain who saw the spectre of his dead sister on a salt pan; all his family saw her sitting there. I have never seen a ghost, but when someone important to me has died, there always seems to be a bird that comes close, or a flock of birds that startle me. A hoopoe long ago. The wren trapped in my husband's studio on the morning after his death. The starlings that filled the ash tree next to my house so that all the branches were flickering with their presence. A friend whose son died said that on the day when he learned what had happened a falcon almost brushed his face with its wings; he had never seen a falcon so close.

Kerry said I had to get to Upington where she had several contacts, and from there it was only a two-and-a-half-hour drive to the area in the Kalahari Desert where she also knew people I should meet. She could not come with me because she had just returned from a trip, but I could easily go on my own, and once again I was back in a truck, my foot on the accelerator, trying to make my determined way to places that were like nothing I had ever seen before. 'You need to speak with the speakers,' she said. 'Don't worry, they will understand a bit of your Dutch and you'll be able to understand enough of their Afrikaans.' She said that there were not many of the old people left, but the ones who were still alive, would want to tell me *dronkverdriet* stories: long, sad, drunken stories about trauma and violence. 'What is your *kuier?*' they will ask, meaning, 'what is your heartache?' And with that you can begin.

In Upington I should try to meet Ivan, the son of Petrus Vaalbooi – *vaal* means tawny, pale or grey, and *booi* means a servant boy. Petrus can be hard work, she said, but his son is very interesting. He studied natural justice, anthropology and law at university in order to be an advocate for his people. I should try to talk to him if he is around, although he might be in the city. I write it all down, but I have no idea which city she is referring to.

Kerry said I had to get to the Kalahari. Take my own water. Five litres. Take a cool box. Take some tobacco, Golden Virginia. Tobacco is called *twak* and the people are used to smoking a very strong mixture called Boxer, but they really appreciate Golden Virginia. Eat at the Diamond Tea House, it's the only coffee shop in the Kalahari, and there is a guest house run by a woman called Hannik, just across the road from the coffee shop. That is where I can stay. It will be very hot, so I'll come out in the morning and hide through the midday and then come out again in the afternoon.

I should try to meet Barbara, a young white woman, and Ivan, her husband, who makes burnt art on bone which they sell from a roadside stall somewhere between Askam and Witdraai, I'll find it easily enough. 'You can stay with them,' says Kerry, 'after you have been at Hannik's.' They have a little boy with green eyes.

Christiana and her husband are somewhere close by and they have a friend called Patac who works on another stall beside the road. He is a very good artist and was hired by the South African state to make the design for the new banknotes, but he remains poor, just like everyone else.

We go on talking and I am persuaded that I can do it all. By the time Kerry is about to leave I feel we have become friends, although goodness knows if I will ever see her again or be able to ask her to clarify some of the more jumbled notes in my notebook.

After she has gone I go for a walk by the sea. There has been a soft scattering of rain. A very battered tortoise sits on the path, masquerading as a stone. The front of his shell looks as if it has been chewed by a dog; perhaps a butcher's dog who wanted sausages but got tortoise instead.

The milkwood trees appear solid and impenetrable, more like huge clumps of moss than trees. When I reach the sea it is very wild, and there is only one solitary surfer being buffeted about. A thick mass of sea woodlice are hopping like big fleas on the wet sand exposed by the receding tide. They eat kelp and in return they are food for the birds. A cormorant skims above the sea's surface with the steady determination of a very slow missile.

I wonder if I would have got to Upington and to the Kalahari if I had been able to stay for the extra two weeks. I like to think I would have done it. I had felt a new sort of courage creeping in on me, alongside the sense that I would be helped by the people I met and I could trust in that.

XXXIV

22 November 2020. When I went up to the studio this morning a male blackbird was sitting very still in the wet grass outside the door. It didn't move as I approached and didn't struggle when I picked it up, but let out a brief burst of noise that was almost a song and almost a cry. The bright yellow rings around its eyes looked as though they had been squeezed from a tube of paint. The black feathers were as soft as wood ash. I lifted one wing and then the other to make sure there was no damage. The tail drooped a bit, but maybe a blackbird's tail does droop. I set the bird down on the grass, where it paused for a moment before lifting into the air and flying away. Bye-bye, blackbird, as the old song goes. My mother used to sing it to me and I sang it to my children.

Trump is out although he is going to fight the fact, while Johnson is still busy with his incongruous metaphors. We are in the midst of this new lockdown. I am in something called Tier Two which means I am allowed to walk with a friend in the fields or by the sea. I sometimes defy the rules that encircle us and invite someone into the house for a cup of coffee and perhaps a biscuit. The silence of the days remains very intense. I often talk to myself out loud but I tend to speak in what I know of French or Dutch or Italian, I suppose because it gives me the sense of a dialogue. I talk to the chickens and the guinea pigs. I apologise to spiders for disturbing them, tell the full moon it is beautiful and mutter my amazement at the drama of a sunset. I think of the Bushmen singing their honey songs to the stars and greeting the jar that is filled with bat-eared fox fat.

After seeing Tim and his family I went back to Cape Town and to my room in Tanya's house. She had developed a noisy cough and cold which did not seem to bother her. She drove me through town to Table Bay, so that I could see the Breakwater jail which is now an expensive hotel near the waterfront. We walked with her dogs along the domesticated coastline and I collected empty limpet shells which are bigger than their European counterparts, with flecked patterns and a sharp outline that made me think of Mount Fuji, not that I have ever seen Mount Fuji. The limpets rattled in my pockets. I gave three of them away when I got back, bestowing them as if they were pearls beyond price. The remaining four sit on the window ledge in the bathroom, looking out on a japonica bush that is often filled with little birds.

The next day I wanted to visit the Cape Town University library, where Tanya had been the head archivist. Ever helpful, she drove me there, passing a spreading township of corrugated-iron roofs pressed together shoulder to shoulder, as if they had grown as lichen grows on a stone, or tiny mushrooms grow on rotting wood.

I was dropped off at the edge of the university complex and I walked in the sunlight along a broad pedestrian way sided by the walls of high brick buildings, sometimes opening up to grand stone staircases that led to other levels and other buildings in the Victorian colonial style. Statues on plinths, but I cannot remember who they were of. It was nice to be moving in a slow river of mostly young people who gave the impression of knowing where they were going and what they were doing.

I found the entrance to the archive department of the Jagger Library. The uniformed attendant behind the desk asked me to sign my name in a book and I was directed up the stairs which I think had white stone steps and mahogany banisters. There was a sort of halfway point with a couple of chairs and a glass cabinet displaying some books whose covers I cannot now see, and then here was the door leading into the library. The hush of academia: everything quiet and patrician; wood panelling on the walls; numbered tables; people concentrating under the glow of individual lamps; the whisper of laptops. A circular desk in the centre for those in charge.

I introduced myself at the desk and chose a table and sat there until the archivist with whom I had been in contact from England came to see me. He was a shy, light-footed, grey-haired man who spoke with a hushed voice as if everything was a secret that must not be overheard by others. He had already sent me the elaborate details of the entire archive, enquiring what I would like to consult, and in return I had made a rather random selection, concentrating mostly on Lucy's work relating to the !Kun boys and some of the early lists of words as a dictionary of /Xam was being pieced together.

The first cardboard boxes filled with notebooks were delivered to my table and that was when my version of Tanya's cold kicked in and I erupted in a quick succession of wet and noisy sneezes. I rushed out to find the ladies' loo from where I could gather some soft lavatory paper because I had no handkerchiefs with me.

Back at my desk I began to skim through the notebooks with their watermarked cardboard covers and black bindings, a little label on the front of each one holding a title followed by intricate reference numbers.

I was looking at one of the earliest of the Breakwater dictionaries compiled by Wilhelm Bleek. The words in English were written on the left side of the page, while a phonetic approximation of /Xam had been written on flimsy pale blue paper and cut into strips and stuck onto the right-hand side. I was startled by the sense of the hugeness of the work that was being undertaken; the act of putting together a complex and unknown language from scratch.

Long ago I had a freelance job compiling the entries for the letters H and L in a new dictionary and I used the same sort of system that Bleek and Lucy were using here, making lists of the words I felt were essential and providing a brief definition that I felt captured the subtleties of their meaning. Once I had completed a section, between life and love perhaps, I cut them into strips and pasted them down on a new page.

The letter K in the /Xam dictionary held the words for to shoot; to run after; to come near; buttocks; black man; slave; bastard. T had *tabaka* – tobacco; *toba* – to work; *tta e* – to run away, along with to get by. Then came to be sore; to be warm; to lie down; vagina; ostrich egg; to pull out; to pull back; to be glad; to be wounded; to be scared. It was like reading a series of abstracted poems following the Haiku rules of *wabi*, *sabi* and *kurumi*: simplicity, lightness and solitude.

I had also ordered the notebook that covered //Kabbo's visit to the Museum of Natural History and when I looked at its cover I found it strangely moving, simply because of the immediacy of the day and the date. The /Xam names for all the living creatures, from a locust to an elephant, somehow gave a different sense of the intimate relationship between these people and the natural world. And again there was the shock of realising the rich diversity of life as it once had been.

For no particular reason I had ordered a notebook called 'Bushmen 334–428 1871 II', in which Bleek was in conversation with //Kabbo while he was still being held in the Breakwater Jail.

The white man has written down everything of mine. He shall go away tomorrow. He shall go to his house. Jackal comes to ask for the dove's child in order to eat it, he kills it in order to eat it.

Who is that? That is Koos Toontje. Who are there? Silo, //Kabbo and Gubri. The trees stand on top of the mountain. The mountain is high.

I knew I should be working here for several weeks but instead I was doing a hit-and-run with just this one day and then a few more days when I returned from the Karoo, perhaps after visiting Upington. For now I kept walking up to the central desk saying I was ready for the next box, and in they came, thick and fast, like the oysters rushing ashore to walk with the Walrus and the Carpenter. I sucked the cough sweets that I happened to have with me and blew my nose into pieces of loo paper, dropping them into a cloth bag with its Edinburgh Festival logo that somehow gave me a sense of street cred. I wanted to explain to the archivist and to the people behind the desk that this was Tanya's cold, not mine. I also wanted to say something about myself and the books I had already written and why I was doing this one and how important it was to me. Instead I bobbed about and apologised for one thing or another and felt like a fool.

I stopped working rather abruptly and returned the last of the boxes to the desk, requesting them to keep everything else I had ordered waiting for me, because I would be back soon. I said goodbye to the archivist, but I have not written to him since, to thank him for his kindness and patience. Perhaps the library has been closed since the end of March.

I needed to catch a bus back to the city centre and I asked a succession of students to help me find the right stop until there it was, with a noisy crowd accumulating around it. When the bus arrived, I clambered in with everyone else and no room to move and students laughing and shouting. I got out at the stop closest to Tanya's road but nothing looked familiar until I was almost in front of her house. I rang the bell and someone appeared out of nowhere and opened the gate for me.

XXXV

3 December 2020. The cold of winter is moving in and when I looked out this morning the grass was coated with a thick and bubbling layer of frost. I have developed the disconcerting habit of reading world news on my iPhone, the screen glistening in my hand in the half-dark so even before I am fully awake I have learned of politicians being political, while fire and contagion sweep across the land, ice sheets melt, the climate spins and oceans accumulate layers of rubbish. Meanwhile I am here in a little house made of wood, doing my best to live correctly, trying to minimise the contents of my recycling bin and remembering to turn off the lights when I go to bed.

Back in Cape Town I was gathering information as fast as I could before setting off for the Karoo. One day I went to the library in the Company's Gardens to see some of the original Bushman drawings from the Bleek Collection. Another dark, high-ceilinged, wood-panelled library in the English Victorian style, lined with leather-bound books and watched over by the white marble busts of important men, all of them looking as if their DNA had been crossed with a succession of nameless Greek gods.

Laddy, the archivist, was very welcoming and there was no need for hushed tones, since no one else was here. He said he hoped that corona would go away soon because he had booked a holiday in April to the Maldives, I think it was. In that still innocent time the word corona made one jump, like hearing a distant explosion of noise that sounded as if it could be gunshot.

Laddy explained that there were very many drawings and watercolour paintings in the collection and it might be best if I began by looking at them on the computer screen. And so I sat in front of the familiar dazzle of technology and scrolled down through images made by /Han‡kass'o and Dia!kwain and by the four young boys who had been bought and sold before they were finally delivered to Lucy in Cape Town. I made a selection of some thirty drawings and waited for Laddy to bring them to my desk.

I had often seen these images in books and articles, but it was different to have them there in front of me. The stained fragility of the sheets of paper. The lines made by a rough-bristled paintbrush, a stubby pencil, a leaking dip pen and the beauty of the drawings themselves, reaching across the dividing line between then and now, confident in their knowledge of animals and birds and trees and people.

Before leaving in what seems to have been my usual flurry, accompanied by a wave of sneezing, I ordered fifty photocopies that I thought I might use in this book and Laddy said he would make sure they were waiting for me when I came back in a couple of weeks.

In the last days before my departure for the Karoo, I became aware that I did not have the right things for the trip. Tanya drove me to the market, both of us talking in a rush of words as we moved deeper into the city traffic. I enjoyed the chaos of the market, the noise of it, the way that those who were selling goods surged towards us as we approached and then pulled back as we passed like waves on a seashore. I bought a rucksack from a man surrounded by rucksacks and the painting of the line of people who seemed to be walking across a desert landscape. I bought trainers and socks, a water bottle and a sun hat and felt I was ready for anything.

That evening Tanya filled me up with propolis tincture and

vitamin C and a frothy mixture she said everyone in South Africa swore by, but when I woke in the morning my head was heavy and my throat was sore and I began coughing like a chain-smoker, making a terrible rattling noise. Tanya assured me that her cold had almost gone and mine would soon follow its example.

At midday I went to meet my fellow travellers at a restaurant. Shyness and courage. The shaking of hands and the brief eye-to-eye gaze to try to glimpse the nature of a stranger. I was to be travelling with Janette Deacon, an archeologist, who has specialised in rock art and the study of the /Xam records. She is a widow now, ten years older than me, very alert and clear-eyed. Also Paul Weinberg, a photographer who has chronicled South Africa's complicated history from the apartheid days to the release of Mandela in 1994 and on into the present. He took a photograph of Mandela putting his voting slip into the ballot box, but the main focus of his work has been the Bushmen, seeing them as they are now in their disenfranchised state: holding on, getting by, sometimes triumphant against the odds and sometimes defeated. A very young naked boy watches a helicopter as it flies close to him like a huge and malevolent insect; big fat tourists take photographs of two emaciated Bushmen who even in the stillness of the image appear to be shivering with hunger and perhaps also with fear; a woman sings; a man and his wife drive a donkey cart. Roger Van Wyk was the youngest of our group. He organises big festivals among other things and had worked with Janette installing the Bushman rock art exhibition at Iziko Museum. This was to be his first visit to the ancient sites in the Karoo.

Three friends. I liked my sense of them but felt I was concentrating too hard in my wish to please, or perhaps to impress. I don't remember what we ate, just that I was trying to explain something about the sort of book I meant to write and how I had come to the idea. My words kept being interrupted by the noisy rattle of the cough – it was as if a stray and mangy dog had attached itself to me and was shadowing me wherever I went.

The next morning I packed the new rucksack with paper handkerchiefs and cough sweets and the propolis tincture and I still have the bottle and the last drops that it holds. Paul arrived in a battered jeep which had cracks in the windscreen and dents in the metalwork and other signs of the dangerous roads it had followed. We collected Roger and set off to the nearby town where Janette lived.

She had previously sent us an itinerary and a map of our journey, along with an estimate of expenses and I wot not what besides. Now there was talk as to whether we should travel in two vehicles or only one, and when I muttered about maybe going on to Upington and Calvinia in pursuit of the list of people I wanted to try to meet, that clinched it, and we decided to crowd in all together in Janette's very un-battered Toyota Land Cruiser.

And then we were off and soon we were travelling along a straight and smooth and well-made road that unrolled itself in front of us in a daze of uniformity. We were crossing a flat expanse of what seemed to be agricultural land dotted with big warehouse buildings for storing produce and smaller buildings for sheltering the people who lived here. I could see fences everywhere: dividing, controlling and containing. No animals, apart from the occasional cluster of sheep.

In trying to remember that trip to the Karoo, it feels as if I was a different person then to the person I am now. I need to make an effort to put myself back in the Toyota, staring out at the country we were moving through. I know it made me think of the Great Western Desert in Southern Australia where the vast area once occupied by the Pitjantjatjara people was used in the 1950s for military experiments, in which dynamite was dropped onto nuclear material, to see what the consequences would be. People spoke of the noise of the explosions, the dark cloud and having to run to save their lives. And once the experimentation was over, high fences were put up to encircle the several thousand square miles that were now contaminated and dangerous to human life.

I remember a woman in the Aboriginal reserve at Yalata lying face down on the grey sand, weeping for the red sand of her childhood.

We drove north for several hours with nothing to distract the eye apart from the occasional white blur of the sheep behind the shining blur of metal fencing. I learned later that these high fences were often electrified at their base, to stop any burrowing animals from getting in.

At a certain point there was a discussion as to whether we should visit the quiver trees forest. That seemed like a good idea and so we left the tarmac and set off on the more tangible reality of dirt roads.

XXXVI

19 December 2020. A new variation of Covid is spreading through the country. My children are marooned in cities that are said to be very dangerous and I will not be able to see them during Christmas. Mohammed cannot go to the mountain and the mountain cannot come to Mohammed.

Today on the radio a very soft-spoken epidemiologist was describing the coronavirus as a creature that wants to survive, just as every living thing wants to survive, ourselves included. She said it would use all its power and subterfuge to achieve that end even though it is such a simple life form, as simple as those tiny organisms that twitched and stirred in shallow water when the life of the world was first beginning to take shape. I do wonder, as we sit on the edge of so much environmental catastrophe, if the world will eventually go back to the minutiae of its own beginning, and then the enormity of time will again kick in and a new trajectory will take shape. Patience and shuffle the cards indeed.

With all these thoughts spinning around my head I walk into the studio and turn on the heater and the laptop and press the blue button on the printer until a green light flickers its willingness to begin. I sit there for a while blankly staring and then I turn off the heater, the printer and the laptop and leave the empty room to its own devices.

I seem to be passing through the days while waiting for some kind of reality to return to me. I had got into the habit of watching lots of films, hardly aware of the difference between one and another, and I had been distracting myself with listening to the radio while taking a bath or eating a meal. When I woke from sleep I stopped my thoughts from rising to the surface, treading them down, locking the door of separation.

But yesterday I defied the ban on movement and went to see a friend who lives on another stretch of coast, north from here. Two hours of driving and two hours of the two of us walking in a wood I had never been to before. It held a number of very old trees, beech mostly, their trunks like elongated human limbs and torsos, their bark as smooth as human skin. Many of the trees close to the path had been inscribed by people who must have had penknives at the ready in their pockets. One patch of bark was slashed with a cross-hatching of angry lines like a multidimensional game of noughts and crosses. One had just the date, 1918, a war coming to an end and maybe this was a way of commemorating its passing.

All the graffiti letters and numbers had been distorted by the energy of the growth of the tree, the scars widening and stretching so that some of them could no longer be identified, while beneath the concealment of the bark, another story was being told in the spinning accumulation of the rings of the seasons, the fat years and the lean years moving through the centuries. On the surface of a grey-green trunk I saw my own initials, JB, and it was as if I had been here long ago and had wanted to state the fact of my existence.

I got lost driving back which is something I do with great ease, my heart racing as if I will never manage to return to the place from which I started. It didn't matter. I had glimpsed a world beyond the strange cage of my immediate surroundings and that made everything OK. I was home before dark had settled and I slept well.

This morning bright sunlight is dancing on the table in front of me that is piled with books and papers, and I am reminded of those eighth-century monks in Ireland bent over their work as they illuminate the words of a new religion on sheets of smooth vellum made from the skins of unborn calves. There they were in their stone cells overlooking the sea and one of the unnamed scribes briefly forgot the haloed saints and the sacred, intricate, curling letters, and wrote in the margin 'how pleasant is the sunlight on this page, for the way it glitters'.

With that image I am ready to return to the Karoo. I see us rattling along the dirt roads until we reached a collection of farm buildings and a smithy from a time when people needed smiths to shoe their horses, but now it had been transformed into a restaurant.

We knocked and the door was opened by an old man who welcomed us as if he had been expecting us. We entered a wood-panelled dining room where the heads of dead animals gazed down from the walls, in the company of the weapons that had killed them. I was shocked yet again by the startling and startled beauty of the varieties of antelope. I think there was also a jackal, along with some old-fashioned farm implements. Big trestle tables were scattered with books, mostly about South African history and botany, and there were more books on shelves along a wall.

The man had been a lawyer but was now retired. He was eager to talk about his knowledge of plants and local history and he also managed to suggest fragments of his own story. There seemed to have been a wife who left him, either by dying, or because she packed her bags and drove away. There were children too, also gone.

We sat at a dark table being entertained by this big-boned and lonely old man who did not want us to ever leave, the tumbling roll of his words leading from one piece of information into the next with no room for interruption or departure. He was like a spider in the web that was his home, waiting for the visits of strangers. We drank a beer and he gave us directions to the Quiver Tree Forest. And then we left and he watched us go.

We drove along rough tracks until we reached a big green metal sign which announced:

Namakwa District Municipality Quiver Tree Forest. Private Property.
– Right of admission reserved.
– Removing/damaging of plant material strictly prohibited.
– Please keep your vehicle to the road.
– No fires.
Conserve our natural heritage for future generations.
Owner. G. J. M. van Wyk

The quiver trees were scattered across a dry hill, carefully distanced one from the next, as we, these days, are supposed to be. The rounded summit of the hill was crowned by what looked like an amphitheatre built from blocks of stone although it had been built by no one but itself. It added to the theatricality of the place, the sense of concentration.

A bright blue sky and the solemn trees that appeared poised and waiting for something to happen. Maybe they were waiting for the /Xam hunters to come back at last, to cut the branches that could be made into quivers for their bows, just as they had always done as the millennia rolled into each other.

Some of the trees were not much taller than me, others were the height of two or three of me standing on my own shoulders. They were utterly still, no fluttering leaves, no twist in the trunk or twitch of movement in the branches that were raised like giant candelabra. It was as if they were caught in a spell that had stopped them in their tracks as they were marching up the hill towards the wall of rock and over it, determined to conquer the dome of the summit.

We were intruders: an audience looking at a stage set, waiting for the action to begin when the /Xam would step out from among the trees; their feet on this hard stony ground protected by shoes made from the skin of anteater, springbok or porcupine. The /Xam talking and laughing together as they cut a few branches from the trees and began to work on them, hollowing them out and turning them into quivers to hold their poison-tipped arrows. A people who belong to a place, a place that recognises its people while we walk about and take photographs, our thoughts distracted.

/Han‡kass'o could be one of the group. He was a hunter and I would say you can see it in his face and the concentration of his gaze, but maybe that sounds disrespectful. He often spoke of the hunt, especially the hunt for springbok. He spoke of the preparation, the watching, the following, the closing in; the rules of behaviour around the person who makes the kill and the rules of behaviour around the distribution of the flesh.

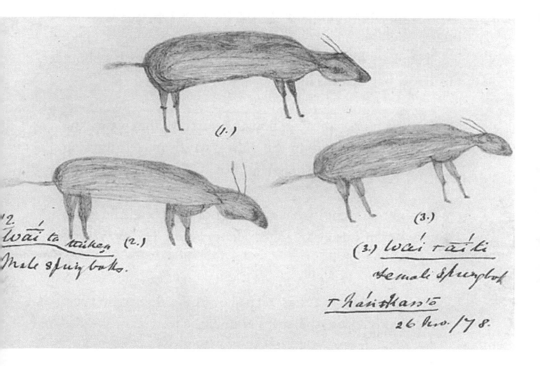

He praised the beauty of the springbok, the way they communicate with each other, the way they move, the interaction between the mothers and their young, the old males and the herd. He could imitate the sounds they made and could describe their movements with flickering gestures of his hands. He would sing songs, a few words that repeated themselves like notes of music.

But whoever was once in this forest, taking a branch for the quiver that would hold the arrows, they left nothing to be remembered by. No scars cut into the trunks. Nothing to say, 'Look at me, I am here and will be here long after I am gone.'

I walk among the trees, watched over by the amphitheatre of rock. The sky is a perfect blue. Nothing moves. I do not even see a bird, although I have read somewhere that the sociable weavers liked to use these branches to hold the weight and structure of their huge nests. Maybe the trees were bigger then, marching for miles across the landscape holding their arms above their heads like Cycladic dancers and the men moving among them, choosing and cutting and hollowing out and binding with thongs made from the skin of the springbok which is the object of the hunt.

/Han‡kass'o slings his newly made quiver on his shoulder. His arrow bag he calls it.

Rattling along, rattling along, the arrows they were, the arrows which were in the quiver, which made a rattling noise because they stirred inside it.

By night he went to make a shelter of bushes and he made a shelter of bushes by night. He lay down. He lay waiting for the springbok.

The springbok that has been shot in the thigh, she runs, she gently goes, she stops running, she walks. She lies down, while she feels that she is faint. Therefore the Bushman, calling in a certain manner, kau wwe kau wwe, while he wishes that the springbok may soon lie down and die for them. That they may eat.

XXXVII

20 December 2020. It's been raining: a heavy, cold, relentless rain. The distinction between the living and the dead has become strangely blurred. I am cut off from the people I love who are in another place to this one where I am: my daughter and her family, my son and his family, my stepdaughter and her daughter in Holland; they all inhabit a world which I am barred from entering. Of course we speak on the phone and meet in those filmed encapsulations that transport us into other rooms at other times of the day and night, but however much I cling to the image of familiar faces and the sound of familiar voices, the sense of separation is huge. By the same strange rules of absence and presence, I am aware of the almost physical reality of those who happen to be dead: my husband, my sometimes mad and bad but curiously honest father, friends disappearing over the years and the three who were swept up when this pandemic had just begun.

It's growing dark outside, not because of the night but because a rainstorm is approaching, thickening the sky with a murky yellow and a grey that is almost black.

The rain lays the great skin along the horizon. It is black.
It comes in the darkness while the people sleep. (//Kabbo)

I turn away from it to watch as I and my three travelling companions leave the Quiver Tree Forest. The towns we pass through remind me of my idea of parts of the American South which I have never seen. A main dirt street, a simple church, a burial ground, postboxes, a few parked cars, silent gardens, fences; everything nonchalantly dropped into a vast and empty land.

We reach the town where we are booked to stay overnight. The two little houses that are our destination stand in a dusty garden behind a low wall. A solitary quiver tree watches the road, missing – or so it seems to me – the sensation of carrying a nest of sociable weavers among its branches, the feel of the backs of antelope rubbing against its smooth trunk. I like to think it also misses the companionship of people like /Han‡kass'o who laughs and sings the pattering music of his songs as he cuts the branch that will make a quiver for the arrows that will shoot a springbok that has agreed to be shot because that is how things once worked.

We each have a room. I have a single bed, an apricot-coloured hand towel carefully folded and placed upon it. A bunch of dried flowers is there to welcome me along with a framed print on the wall which shows a coastline, or a waterfall, or perhaps it is an elephant. The woman who owns the houses comes by to check that we have everything we need and then drives off to her husband and family in some other little town not very far away and probably not very different to this one.

I walk across the road to the Baptist church which has been turned into a museum. A wooden board divided into a grid that once held the hymn numbers to be sung on each new day of the week, now holds the phone number of a woman called Aletta and another called Annette. The board has in turn been hammered onto a white metal sign, leaving just enough room for the words printed at the top of it: *Open For Accompa.n. Tours 9vm–5nm Mon–Sat*. A little crowd of quiver trees are standing about in the company of a number of wind pumps. It looks as if they have agreed to a symbiotic relationship, rooted in the same hard ground. No sound. No wind. Nothing moves, not even a dog or a cat.

Paul and Roger have arranged what is called a braai. They light the outside barbecue and we drink beer while it heats up and then we eat chops and sausages and drink more beer and talk convivially in the gathering dusk. My sneezes and the cough have temporarily subsided. An almost full moon hangs in the sky above us.

> The moon is a thing which knows things, for it sees things
> that will come to pass. It is the one who knows the things
> that we do not know. (Dia!kwain)

I slept well, but when I woke, although the sneeze had diminished, the cough had returned and as horrible as ever. Janette came into my room to tell me that a lockdown had been declared across the whole country and maybe we should cancel our trip, but without much further discussion we decided to continue. The four of us ate breakfast, packed our things and set off along more juddering dirt roads, before grinding to a halt with a flat tyre which was something to do with the air pressure being too high for such rough surfaces. While the others replaced the tyre I hovered about and photographed the apparition of a few tiny yellow flowers erupting like a miracle from the dry dust and grit.

We approached the area where the young Dia!kwain used to live with aunts and uncles and cousins, an elder brother and two sisters: /A-kumm, the Story of a Fight, and Whai-ttu, Springbok Skin. His mother was /Ko:ang, or Start Back, because of the surprised way she reacted whenever she was spoken to. His father Xaa-ttin died when Dia!kwain was only fourteen years old, but in spite of his death he never really went away, remaining as his son's closest companion up until the end.

mama kan /au: my mother
ibo kan /au: my father

n'ga kan au: my brother
n'kappa kan au: my sister

Dai!kwain said that in a time before the Boers, Xaa-ttin chipped the images of gemsbok, quagga, ostrich and people into the round dolerite stones that we are now going to visit. I wonder if meeting the stones will be something like meeting Xaa-ttin.

And now we are at a metal gate flanked by metal fences and opening onto the track to a farm called Varskans, the name taken from the /Xam *!kann*, meaning spring. A yellow metal sign of ownership is fixed to the gate and its words of prohibition are illustrated with the black outline of a skull and crossbones, a snarling dog, a gun, a bolt of electricity and a pair of handcuffs, one cuff ready to be snapped shut on a wrist. In Afrikaans and in English I read, 'Warning. Access Prohibited. Any person entering this area without proper authority exposes himself to danger and prosecution. Distributed by Philip du Toit, copyright John Wright.' The location, in case you need to call the police for more dogs and guns and handcuffs, is 'BW08 Bravo 202'. Mr Wright's cellphone number is also included, so you can contact him if you want to order another sign.

The gate was supposed to have been left open for us, but it is firmly locked. Janette phones the farmer and a white truck starts to move towards us over the rough land. A strong-bodied and stocky man steps out of the truck and introduces himself as Klaas.

Klaas returns to his farm while we walk up to the crest of the hill, or *brinkkop* as it is called in Afrikaans. There are no paths, but patches of hard sandy earth are exposed in between the scrubby bushes. No sign of any animals, not even a footprint or a whitened bone, just the ticking of red-winged grasshoppers and the nostalgic squeak of unseen birds. A lazy fly, mosquito larva in a shallow pool of water from the recent rain. Soft wind and the absurdity of so many fences, and now we are approaching the top of the hill and we are surrounded by the black and glistening boulders of dolerite. As I walk among them, I feel as tiny and insignificant as an ant. Many of the boulders are just their una-dorned selves, but then I begin to see that one and another and yet another has an image cut into its shining surface.

Here are human figures dancing around a beautiful eland, the creature immediately recognisable from the position of the horns and the humped curve of the shoulders. The eland always had a close connection with the rain. By the time the /Xam replaced the First at Sitting People, the eland had become the Rain Bull, or the Water Cow, depending on who was speaking of him.

> A man, I do not know his name, but he was one of the First at Sitting People and he hunted the Rain, as the Rain was grazing there. The Rain was like an eland.

> My mother told me that people pull out the Water Cow, and lead her over to their place, so rain will fall on their place and the !kaui wild onion leaves will come out, and then the people will live and if the rain does not quite fall then the people will die.

> My father Xaa-ttin said the people went near the water spring, which has a great and deep hole or pit. The Water Bull was in the place. And they felt the wind seemed to beat them, so the Water Bull might not smell them and they might go to the water and lie in wait for him . . . that they might pull the thong tight upon his head when he came, to take him away with them. (Dia!kwain)

In the drawing on the rock I can see the thong around the neck of the eland, and I can see the cut marks on his neck and the lines of something that must be his blood, bursting from the body and fall-ing like rain on the ground, while the people dance around him.

A horse runs across the smooth surface of another boulder.

Or is it a quagga? I remember Dia!kwain saying that the quagga was once so tame that you could go up to it and stroke it, until a man from the Early Race of the First at Sitting People hit it with a stick to teach it fear, so that it might run away when hunters came. He should have hit it more violently, imbued more terror into it, and then it might have outlived those first encounters with men and their guns. It was Dia!kwain who said, 'wild quagga weep if one of their own is wounded. They cry and make a noise together if they smell of the scent of blood.'

I walk among the silent boulders. Living here, Dia!kwain and his people were much too close to the Sak River which formed the border with the Cape Colony. The Trekboers, known as *baan-brekers*, or breakers-through of paths, were steadily exploring and making claim to this area where the Bushman grass was said to grow like wheat in the wind and game was so abundant. That is why Dia!kwain's family had knives and tinderboxes and his mother had a European needle, all evidence of trade between the /Xam and the Boers. It is also why he saw so much death while he was still young. The mist of battle. The savagery of killing. The punishment for eating the meat of a sheep or a bullock when there was no other food to be found. 'Is it such a big thing what we have done?'

When he was about eleven years old Dia!kwain became very ill. His mother took him to a sorcerer woman who was called Mietje, an Afrikaans name even though she spoke no Afrikaans. She explained that in this time of turmoil, 'our people who used once to be sorcerers seem to be dying off, taking their thoughts away from us. We call to the sorcerers without getting an answer from them.'

It was understood that Dia!kwain's illness was caused by the sorcerers who were dead and who wanted to take him into their land of the dead and maybe keep him there, but his mother refused to let them have her son and so he recovered.

We walk down towards the farm named after the spring from

which Dia!kwain and his family used to get their water. We are welcomed by a big friendly dog. The garden has raised flower beds and a fountain in a courtyard, which might be fed by Dia!kwain's spring but I do not ask. Klaas and Janette speak together for a while, and before we leave he says he wants to show us something and he leads us to a hangar which houses a huge lorry and machines for grappling with the land.

At the back of the hangar there is a long shelf on which he has placed a collection of ostrich eggs. He came across them when he was excavating a patch of land with a digger. He offers an egg to me and one to Roger. I hold my one very carefully, admiring its smoothness, its lightness and the perfect symmetry of the round hole at its top, cut I suppose by someone within Dia!kwain's family group. Each egg would have been filled with water and sealed with beeswax before being hidden in a place where it could be found in a time of drought.

> The people made for her a reed which she might drink with. She must drink with a reed placed in the mouth of the ostrich shell, the egg shell with a small hole, so that only a little water may come through. (Dia!kwain)

But although drought must have often visited the land during the intervening years, the people whose land it was did not return. Dia!kwain's father was dead, his mother had vanished, Mietje's husband and young son were shot by the Boers while they were collecting the poisons to prepare the arrows for the springbok hunt. A few others survived, but they had to dip down, dip down and scatter.

Dia!kwain's parents had tried to protect their children, 'because they felt we must ourselves seek food, feeding ourselves. While they felt that they would dying go away from us and leave us and we must not think that other people who are different to us, would be those to give us food.'

But how do you find food when there is no food to find, apart from the forbidden sheep and the forbidden cattle?

Klaas regards his cache of ostrich eggs with something like reverence and something like confusion. 'You can have them,' he says, pleased with the thought of giving away these things that belong to none of us.

The anteater said, 'Bushmen shall eat meat which is cooked in a fire. Bushmen shall light fires. They shall also boil in a pot. They shall also drink water from ostrich shells. (/A!kunta)

I am aware of my eagerness to take what is offered: a smooth white sphere stained with brown swirls of colour from the earth in which it has been lying. I would have brought it back with me, wrapped even more carefully than the abalone shell, and I would have given it a place of honour, here in my house. However, Jan ette was very quick in refusing such gifts on behalf of all of us, and that was it. A clutch of empty eggs remain in a dark shed, at home and yet far from home.

Looking at the photograph of Dia!kwain taken in Mowbray, I try to shake off the intervening years, the Western clothes, his almost European manner, the pipe that he is smoking and the fact of his death when he had not yet reached the age of forty. I make him young again in the company of his people. The eland has been pulled from the waterhole and a soft rain has been persuaded to fall and Dia!kwain is stepping among the boulders on the *brink-kop*, looking down at the flat lands where the grass will again grow like wheat in the wind and the grass eaters and the eaters of meat will be abundant.

XXXVIII

28 December 2020. From this window I can see the broccoli plants in the vegetable bed I dug when I first came back from South Africa; a little patch of cultivated earth that has been part of my daily life for almost a year now. Sometimes it has appeared in my eyes as exquisite as a medieval embroidery celebrating the movement of the seasons in leaf and flower, but it can also be nothing more than a jumble of bedraggled plants, struggling to survive.

Today I am proud of my broccoli. It has come into its own, tilted at funny angles by the weight of dark leaves that promise to feed me even if there is snow on the ground. The spinach is less hopeful; it has persevered but has transformed itself into a mass of tough and branching stems. The garlic cloves might or might not be growing fat beneath the soil. The leeks remain thin, but I should probably start to eat them before their thinness becomes woodiness. The broad beans – the few that were not dug up and devoured by mice – look exhausted. The lettuces have withstood the frost; they are small, battered, resilient and very muddy. However much I wash them, I taste the earth and feel the grit between my teeth.

Yesterday I was watching a YouTube interview between the film director David Lynch and a Georgian journalist. She had a fragile birdlike head and long straight hair that moved a lot as she spoke, while his heavy head showed the chiselled solidity of the bones beneath the skin and the mane of white hair appeared stiff and curiously lifeless.

She drank water and he drank beer and smoked cigarettes and there they were sitting by a window at a table in a cafe with people close by, but no other voices intruded on their conversation. At one point Lynch said, 'The idea is always way different from the words, but you must write the words down to keep you from forgetting the idea,' and I wrote his words down, so as not to forget them.

It's the same with dreams, and as I write this I suddenly remember something of a dream from last night which I had forgotten because I was too lazy to switch on the light and fetch a notebook and a pencil. In the fragment that comes back to me I was hiding under a big bed with a dog, the wonderful thin and golden dog I still miss twenty years or more after his death, and then he and I went out into the dark streets and something happened but I no longer know what it was, except that the dream was about the pandemic and how much it frightens me, and the dog was there to share my fear, or perhaps to ignore it and so make it less dangerous.

Recently I got into a terrible muddle because I had lost all recollection of the next place we visited in the Karoo. According to the itinerary of the trip, we saw Dia!kwain's childhood home and then drove north until we reached the area known as !Njarries where he was living with his wife and three children, along with ǂKasin, and his wife and three children, and two other families. They were based not far from a waterhole fed by an underground spring, and although the spring had dried up by the 1940s, you could apparently still locate their camp from the thorn bushes marking the site of where it had been, and you could look through the bushes for a glimpse of a flat slate of rock over which the water once ran.

This little group were six or eight kilometres from where the farmer Jacob Kruger and seven other families had pitched their tents by a salt pan and a waterhole and where later there would be a farm known as Gifvlei, or Poison Pond, maybe because of the arrows used by the /Xam. We must have had permission to enter the land, but I didn't remember going through a gate, although I had a dim recollection of walking up the side of the hill and reaching the absent spring, and I was quite sure I had looked down at a man-length pile of black boulders marking the place where Jakob Kruger was buried. I found it odd that I had made no notes about the visit, but maybe that was simply because we were in a hurry and I forgot.

I became dizzy from the effort of searching my memory, no longer sure what was real and what was imagined, and so I wrote to Janette and she explained that we never got to !Njarries because of the flat tyre. Apparently the farmer with the ostrich eggs had arranged for a new tyre to be waiting for us in Kenhardt, and then we continued without stopping until we reached the town.

But even though I did not see the place where a little group of hungry people were trying to live, I think I can see Jakob Kruger approaching on his horse. I am helped by a portrait photograph of him and his wife. She is dressed in traditional Dutch costume and is wearing a necklace that could be made of little garnets, similar to the one my Dutch mother-in-law gave me that dates from this same period. He is in black with a white collar and there is a white sweep of something across his chest that might be a watch chain. They both stare at the camera's eye with what looks like an angry and Calvinistic gaze of righteousness. Jakob has dark hair and a beard which seems to be hiding a rather weak chin – or is that my imagination?

Anyway here he comes, bobbing through the driedoring bushes in the middle of the day, intent on his purpose. He knows Dia!kwain and the others because they have bartered goods with each other: a load of wood in return for tobacco and the sweet dumplings the Dutch are very fond of, and another exchange in which the /Xam received fresh ammunition for their guns.

There is no way of knowing if Dia!kwain and his people had stolen the six missing sheep – they might have simply wandered off and been taken by jackals. The only evidence was a skeleton that had been found a few kilometres away, but Kruger was confident in his accusation and the people were hungry, which could in itself be seen as proof of their guilt.

> He sits. He cannot speak for hunger. He cannot stand up for hunger. (/A!kunta)

Keeping to his horse, he accused Dia!kwain and ‡Kasin of the theft and did not accept their denials but said he would come back with an armed commando to wreak vengeance. As he left Dia!kwain shot him in the back.

In that moment of confrontation Dia!kwain must have seen the dream of his father's death in which a different Boer said he would kill Xaa-ttin for killing a sheep and Dia!kwain asked if what had been done deserved such a punishment. In the dream he offered to work for the Boer, to pay for the cost of the sheep. But what happened next, outside the dream, is not clear, apart from the fact that Xaa-ttin died soon after. Now Dia!kwain was surely thrown back to the memory of his father's death and all the other acts of violence he had witnessed throughout his life. It might be that he asked Kruger for leniency and it was not given or he did not ask and simply shot the man who meant to kill him and his people.

In the photograph of Dia!kwain taken when he was at Mowbray I am struck by the fact that he is smiling to himself, as if he is thinking of something that pleases him. I wonder if the smile comes from the knowledge that he did the right thing: one death as an answer to so many deaths and never mind the consequences.

> The men lay dead. And he saw that a Boer commando must have been those who killed the people . . . And that was why the the men did not return . . . And another woman said: 'Leave the sheep's fat on the white-breasted crow's neck, for it was he who came to tell us nicely about it, that our menfolk are all murdered.'

XXXIX

2 January 2021 and as a way of welcoming this new year I sent a photo to a German friend of my cockerel balancing precariously on a post with its beak open in the act of crowing. He replied with a translation of a rhyme he had learned as a child in Berlin in the 1940s: 'When the cock crows on the dungheap, the weather will change, or remain as it is.'

I wake in the silence of the night or I'm startled by my solitude in the silence of the day, and I try to distance myself from the uncertain future by returning to the past with thoughts of the /Xam and the places in which they lived and died.

Having not visited the hillside where the man called Dia!kwain killed the Boer called Jakob Kruger, we drove towards our next destination. Stopping for petrol on the way, a sudden crowd of young boys surged around the truck. Some just stared at us, or held out a hand begging for money to be placed in the palm, while others muttered a repetitive incantation, 'Hungry, hungry, hungry.' I sat there cocooned by metal and glass, and even though I was ashamed of being so impassive, I allowed myself no connection with these people whose faces were close to mine. I suppose I do the same in big cities, bestowing a benevolent coin or keeping it in my pocket, as the mood of confusion takes me.

We reached Elrina's mother's house in the town of Kenhardt

which was called !Kau-/nunu, before the white men's houses came. There the two of them were waiting to take us to the family farm of Arbeidsvreug – the Joy of Work – on the land that once belonged to //Kabbo and his fathers before him.

Their place it is not; for //Kabbo's father's father's place it was. And then it was //Kabbo's father's place when //Kabbo's father's father died. //Kabbo's eldest brother died and then it was //Kabbo's place . . . Our grandfather did walk about this ground . . . Our grandfather did think that our grandfather's father's place it is . . . Therefore our grandfather's father did dying leave it to our grandfather.

I'd had a lot of email communication with Elrina before I left for Cape Town. She wrote of her love for the farm where she had been brought up. She said her father Nak, who died not long before, had taught her everything he knew about the land and the traces it held that bore witness to the life of //Kabbo and his people. In the week before my flight she let me know that soft rain had fallen; not much, but it was the first rain for eight years.

When I was at my place I used to dream. I dreamt that I told the rain to fall for me, for my arm ached and my chest ached. Therefore I dreamt that I spoke and the rain agreed to fall for me, for the rain felt I was dying of thirst and must drink. Then the rain fell and I drank, because the rain helped me.

People say there is no scent so sweet as rain. Therefore the people say it is fragrant.

She said that as she wrote she could see clouds gathering in the sky and she hoped there would be more rain. The desert would come alive, plants that had lain dormant erupting out of the red sand and

231

bursting into flower. There would be birds and maybe animals as well. She looked forward to showing me the beauty of it all. She sent a photograph in which the sun was setting across a wide land in a fanfare of colours, a wind pump in the foreground.

> I told my grandfather that the earth was dry. All places were dry. The bushes were dry. The grass was dry. I had to travel away from the old water whose water was not sweet. I travelled with the springbok to the sweet water pool. I travelled to where the flowers were on the bushes.

Elrina had work in Upington and she lived there with her husband and two children. Since Nak's death, her mother Alma had not wanted to live alone on the farm and had moved to this house.

> After father had died, leaving us, the springbok passed the hut as if they were not afraid. Mother did not know where they came from. They were not few. They came and played as they approached the hut where father lay dead. (Dia!kwain)

Alma had brought her memories with her: the garden filled with stones collected from that other place. Round black dolerites the size of cannon balls surrounded the perimeters of the flower beds in the company of angular and more complicated stones with bright colours zigzagging across them. Each succulent plant that had been persuaded to cling to life was encircled by a ring of white quartz, and a single quiver tree had a dense scattering of flat brown stones placed around its trunk. If you were to come to this garden without knowing anything about it, you might think it was a shrine to unknown gods. And I suppose it was in a way: a shrine for //Kabbo and his people and for Elrina and Alma's people too.

We sat drinking beer on a covered terrace looking out at the garden and Elrina's young son was there and her husband came by. Alma seemed wrapped in a private grief, but maybe it was also her shyness.

Elrina offered to sort out the tyre and I asked if I could go with her. We began by driving a short way to what appeared to be a township within the town, where people drifted out of tin shacks and sat in the dust and half-naked children walked on bare feet. We collected a man from one of the shacks who knew how to mend the tyre and took him to the house of a woman who had the tools necessary for doing the work. She was thin and pale, her wispy blonde hair pulled severely back into a ponytail and a sort of nervous fury in her movements and her voice. Her son watched us with a listless intensity. I had a sense of the strict hierarchy within this remote community where everyone was powerless in one way or another.

Returning to Elrina's mother's house, we stopped at a cemetery surrounded by a flimsy wire fence that would not keep anyone in or out. The land was as it were embroidered by the same delicate yellow flowers I had seen by the roadside and a scattering of graves lay among the creeping flowers. Each grave was nothing more than a person-sized heap of red earth, held in place by flat black stones, with no indication of who was lying where, or when they had lived and died; nothing but these simple floating beds for the dead. Elrina said the graves were old but she did not know how old. A few more modern ones lay around the outer perimeter of the cemetery and they had cement crosses standing at the head of the covering of black stones.

The Moon said, 'When I am dead I return and am again living.' The Moon said, 'I had intended that you who are people should be like me, not altogether dying when you die, but coming back as I do. I had thought to give you this.' But because of the hare who thought his mother

233

was altogether dead and did not believe she only slept, the Moon became angry. Because of the hare the moon cursed us and now we die altogether and vanish. (Dia!kwain)

We also stopped at a bottle store which was nothing more than a shed with a rough counter within its dark interior. Elrina was buying plastic bags filled with ice, because there was no electricity at the farm. She was served by a tiny old man who had only one front tooth and he was so frail he seemed to be almost without a body, and yet there was a fluid grace in his movements. He carried the bags of ice to the truck. He took the battered paper notes that paid for them. He smiled and said thank you and had that same distant gaze I kept seeing in the photographs of the /Xam, a distance that kept him safely beyond the pain of any defeat.

Once the tyre was fixed we set off to Joy of Work, following bumpy dirt tracks as the evening began to draw in. I sat with Elrina in her truck, getting out to open one gate and then another, and finally we were approaching the house and I could see the wind pump I had seen in the photograph and the bulk of a sociable weavers' nest on an electricity pole that was no longer used. We went inside a simple, white-painted building. The oil lamps were lit. I was shown my room.

Elrina had already told me that I would be given the room in which her father had died. For the final two months Nak had been paralysed after a heart attack, but Elrina still managed to drive him around the land and he confided in her the last of the secret places he had discovered where he thought there might be /Xam artefacts. She held on to everything he told her, as an aspect of her love for him. Half jokingly she said maybe I would meet his ghost in his bedroom and half jokingly I said I hoped so.

The curtains in the room were dark red and shiny and looked as if they might suddenly swing open for the first act of an opera. The bed itself had a silky purple covering, embroidered with swirling patterns and the pillowcases were in the same material. I had an oil lamp by the bed, along with a little metal pot of Zam-Buk balm, *the hospital in your pocket*, and a citronella candle against the mosquitoes. Elrina left me to unpack. When I sat on the bed, I could see myself sitting on the bed in a long mirror fixed to the wardrobe.

That evening we said grace before eating lasagne and sweet potatoes wrapped in pastry and cooked with sugar. Alma still seemed distant and abstracted and Elrina watched over her, encouraged her, kept her with us.

We all took turns in the little bathroom and were careful with the water which was in short supply. I dosed myself with paracetamol and the propolis tincture and put the Zam-Buk balm on my lips and around my sore nostrils in the vague hope that I would be better in the morning, and then I made my way to the bedroom in which Elrina's father died. The wind pump kept up the steady breathing of a large animal all through the night, or maybe it was the ghost of the old farmer called Nak who was taking such big and laboured breaths. I think I heard an owl. I slept well and dreamt of my husband.

The hammerkop bird, whose cry is kak/yaak, when a star has fallen it flies over us, it cries. It comes to tell us that our person is dead . . . it sees all things. It lives in the water. (Dia!kwain)

XL

7 January 2021. Last night was the storming of the Capitol in Washington. Trump spoke to his people from behind a protective screen and the whispering intensity of his voice was something you might expect from a zombie in an old horror film. His followers were extras in the same film: men and women filled with an incoherent rage, one of them was dressed in a wolf suit with Viking horns on his head and tattoos across his bare chest and stomach, although he was not as blankly terrifying as some of the others. I sat up in bed and watched them on my iPhone as they rampaged through the rooms of state and it was like watching the spread of the virus embodied in human form.

In the morning I briefly forgot what I had seen and then I remembered and was shocked all over again by the storm of the world, pounding like waves on the shore of my life and all our lives. And that evening, talking to the friend in Berlin who told me of the cockerel on the dungheap, I had a tickling cough as if I had inhaled a mouthful of dust, and although the cough disappeared I was restless through the night and woke with a headache and thought I was about to die. I spoke to a Covid helpline official in Fife who wrote down my details and said he'd read a couple of books by someone with that same name and when I told him it was me he said I'd made his day, which was such a nice thing to hear that the headache vanished with the reassurance of existing in some shape or form beyond the strange ghost I feel I have become.

Meanwhile, on 17 March 2020 we all gathered rather haphazardly for breakfast in the morning: friendly and yet distant and yet friendly. I wandered out to look at what was left of //Kabbo's world and was confronted by a precarious desolation. Structures that must have been erected for a clear purpose had collapsed, their purpose gone. A concrete platform that once held a heavy machine needing just such a platform was now host to plastic canisters, broken floor tiles and a rusting lump of metal I couldn't identify. A bit further on I came across a hand-operated washing machine complete with mangle, lying on its side like a dead thing. In one of her many vivid stories about her family and her life, Elrina told me that her grandmother once found a red diamond lying on the red sand, but she sold it immediately because they were poor and needed the money.

I think of myself in the lockdown that descended like a cage last year: struggling to build a chicken run with the knowledge that no one could come and help me do it, mending the wooden steps that lead to the upper level of this garden by jamming bits of brick under the rotting treads, balancing on a child's chair while trying to fix the bird table and hurting my knee when I toppled off. The shed which now holds the guinea pig hutch because it is too cold outside also holds a growing heap of rubbish that needs to be taken to the dump, but the dump is closed. I struggle in something like the same way that Elrina and her family have struggled.

I once lived on a farm in Suffolk that was empty for thirty-five years before we moved in. The farmer who owned it had lived here as a child and even though his memories were of extreme poverty he said it was where he had been most happy, and that was why he kept it and watched over it. Concrete had been poured in a drift across part of the ground floor, so that he could store sacks of

237

fertiliser, pesticides and rat traps. One of the upstairs bedrooms were littered with shit and feathers from the geese that were kept there for a while, and I liked to imagine them craning their necks out of the windows that still held thin curtains. An elegant chaise longue in the kitchen collapsed into dusty fragments of itself when I touched it.

After he married and moved to another village, the farmer went on cultivating the land he loved with a fierce passion, but when the government offered him a grant for ripping up hedges, cutting down trees and filling in a pond or two, he did as he was told because he was an obedient man, and so it was that step by step over the years he created whatever is the opposite of an oasis. Nettles and brambles surged across the garden and the fields were lifeless apart from the single crop they were growing. The barn where a barn owl used to have its nest now gave shelter to rotting hay and rat poison. Bundles of barbed wire were stored in the kitchen along with an assortment of plastic canisters and sacks and bottles all containing powerful chemicals. I remember reading the list of what would be destroyed by one particular herbicide and it was like a magical inventory of wild flowers from an old meadow. The farmer told me the poisons he was using often made him feel ill and yet he went on using them.

Arbeidsvreug, the Joy of Work, covers an area of fourteen by fourteen kilometres. Elrina's father's father took it on from someone else, but I think the family were here right at the start when the Boers were first making claim to the land of the /Xam. They were sheep farmers and the survival of the sheep was the only thing that made the survival of the farm possible. Until recently they still had a thousand sheep but then the drought kicked in and now the land could only support 120 animals and even those numbers were diminishing.

The Boer had been beating him about herding the sheep,
that he had not herded the sheep well. (Dia!kwain)

238

I saw no sheep in the vicinity of the house, but everywhere I looked I saw evidence of them. The dusty soil was pockmarked by the passing of their sharp feet and scattered with dried clumps of their excrement. Fragments of their bones and skulls had been bleached as white as snow and I was briefly transfixed by a twisted parcel of skin that had once been a newborn lamb.

I drifted back to the farm and we set off in two vehicles to Bitterpits which //Kabbo had spoken about so often. We drove over untracked sand and scrub and through a few gates, and we were always surrounded by metal fences to hold life in and to hold life out. I was with Elrina in her truck. She told me that when the electric generator was still functioning her father had laid electrified wires at the base of the fences to stop any digging animals from getting through, and that was how he first discovered there were hedgehogs on the land, because he found them lying dead, alongside a number of tortoises. He made the effort of lifting the wires a bit above the ground so perhaps the hedgehogs and the tortoises could manage, even though the jackals and the caracal cats, the porcupines and the meerkats, and many other creatures could not.

As we approached the Bitterpits, the fleeting figure of a meerkat paused to rise up on its haunches to look at us when Elrina whistled to it. 'Go back! Go back!' cried a clatter of grouse, and we also saw a black-and-white bird from the bustard family, known here as *korhaan brandgat*, which made a whirring electric sound of surprise as it rose into the air, before sinking silently to the earth with the plummeting descent you might expect from a falling stone.

So here we were at the Bitterpits which //Kabbo knew as //Xara-//kam. I had seen an old black-and-white photograph which had lodged itself in my mind, but what I saw now was nothing like what I was expecting. In the photo, there was a gathering of flat rocks, pitted with marks that were surely made by human hands, and the rocks seemed to stand guard over the ancestral water source that had survived for thousands of years.

He waits for the return of the moon, that he may return, that he may look around the water pits that he did drink from . . . that he may gather together his children, that they put his water pits in order, for he did go away from the place.

What I was now looking at was a half-broken cistern made of concrete and breeze blocks and covered over with planks of wood and sheets of corrugated zinc. Peering down through a gap, I could see the gleam of what must have been water, way below. An old plastic pipe, which once held and perhaps still held a bee colony, carried a little drip of water from the pit to a metal drinking trough with a ballcock device to replenish the water that had been drunk. //Kabbo spoke of the colony of bees at the Bitterpits, so maybe their descendants were somewhere here in a new and more modern home.

The people beat the drum so the bees may be many, so the people can eat honey. The people take the honey to the women, for the women are dying of hunger. When the women have eaten the honey they make a drum for the men, so the men can dance. The men dance while the women sit down and clap their hands, while one woman beats the drum. (/Han‡kass'o)

The ground around the trough was wet and covered with a thin film of green slime. The dusty surface of the land was thick with sheep shit and marks of the movement of sheep. I tasted a drop of water from the trough and it was indeed bitter.

XLI

9 January 2021. Yesterday I went for a walk by the sea with a friend and the air was thick with mist and the sea was buffeting and jostling towards the shore in long angry waves. But then the sun came through and we were surrounded by a buttery light, the kind of light that William Blake used for Heaven and its inhabitants.

When I went to bed last night I kept making an almost imperceptible slide between my thoughts and my dreams, so that I could not distinguish one from the other. Today the air is still and the frost that covered the grass and the branches of trees is melting under the bright gaze of sunlight. I am surrounded by an intensity of silence, not even broken by the robin who often sings in the face of everything and sometimes sits on the handle of the glass door, peering into this room.

After the Bitterpits we went in search of the dwelling sites where //Kabbo had lived with his family. The people always chose to sleep on the lower sandy areas below the hills, because in the high places the lightning was attracted to the volcanic rocks and there could be as many as four fiery strikes during a single storm.

Elrina followed a complicated route, driving over metal fences where they had been flattened sometime before. And then we stopped and she and Janette walked this way and that, scouring the ground for the tiny traces of the past that would tell them if they were close to what they were looking for. As we moved and stared and stopped and moved again, I was aware of Elrina's sense of being part of the lineage of this place and there was an intensity about her, as if she was back with her father and together they were reading the signs and traces that would connect them with the /Xam.

By now a wind was blowing. The midday sun was very hot and I was coated with a layer of salt and sand.

> The sun crossed over. It stood. It went into the sky when it was hot. While our head shadows were long our head hair became long, it stood upright like blades of grass. Our head hair shadow was short in the morning, it had become long while we were sitting in the noonday's shade. (/Han‡kass'o)

Many of the bushes had died in the drought, but others had responded to the recent rain with a soft tinge of green. There were fragile flowers, sky blue and yellow and white, but I did not see a living thing anywhere, apart from the swirling trail left by a little snake in the sand.

> The place becomes dry, therefore the Bushmen become dead on account of it, if the rain does not fall and the springbok are not there, and the locusts vanish. The Bushmen eat !gambro whose plants are there. The !kouwih plants vanish. The !gambro is dry and therefore the !gambro intoxicates us. It kills some people. (/Han‡kass'o)

Elrina pointed out the thin stalk of a bitter gourd that held enough liquid to save someone's life, and she gave me a few of the dusty and woolly leaves from a buchu plant to chew, my mouth intrigued by the powdery texture and the lingering taste of something like bread. The sage-green tips of the buchu plant had a sharper, saltier taste that was just as surprising.

We were there for an hour or it might have been two, and every so often Janette and Elrina would stop and consult each other before going on. Elrina said her father saw himself as a guardian of the land and he wanted to keep people away from this site and even she had only been brought here occasionally as a special favour. Perhaps he did not want us here and that was why she couldn't find the area she was looking for.

Then we came across the big egg-shaped white quartz stone that /Han‡kass'o had described as being close to a dry riverbed, although I could see nothing that looked as if it had ever been a river. The stone was big enough to stand on and an important landmark in such an unmarked area. Janette was busy among the bushes beyond the stone and there she found a group of dwellings which I would never have recognised for what they were until she pointed out some round black stones that must have once leaned against the branches that formed the structure of a group of simple shelters. But the stones had been scattered and they no longer drew the shape of a circle. It might have been that this was where //Kabbo lived in the time before the death of his father, and then after the death they moved on, putting a little distance between themselves and the body of the dead man.

He quickly died and the people buried him and he is said to have said singing, 'the old pot must remain, the old pot must remain, the old bedding must remain.' He said the people must leave some things for him, 'for I lie in the old house' for he felt he must inhabit the house in which he had died. (/A!kunta)

grave
earth
tree

243

the dead man's bag placed under his head
the chamber where the body is placed. (Tamme)

The wind had risen up more strongly and I thought of the wind that comes to blow away the footprints of the /Xam, so that it no longer seems as if they still live.

Elrina was calling for us to come because she had just found //Kabbo's place, the place to which he longed to return. I thought of !Nanni talking with his grandfather, the two of them sitting together in a gathering of little huts, the fires burning, the dead close by, his mother and father far away, trying to find food.

> //Kabbo's brother dying, //Kabbo possessed the place . . . he did growing old, sit with his wife at the place, while his children did married sit at the place . . . while my house did stand alone in the middle, while my children did live on either side.
>
> Then autumn will quickly be upon us when I am sitting at my own place, the name of which I have told you. You know it. You wrote it down. My name is beside my place.

I could see the same cabbage-sized black stones that must have been brought down from the hilltops, but here they denoted the perfect circularity of four dwellings that had been built of branches covered over with leaves and grass or animal skins.

> That wind which does not a little blow, it is the one that lies in the east. It is cold. Therefore the Bushmen make bush shelters. They light a fire. They sit to warm themselves. They sit sheltered there. They sit kkun ssho.

Shelters like bird's nests on the ground, providing only the slightest defence from anything, from everything. At night a jackal sniffs the presence of people.

> If a jackal thought that it would come and take us out of sleep, that it should smell the scent of the fire, it should think that a man was still awake.

Although perhaps it is not a jackal, but a sorcerer, filled with nostalgia for the time when he was still alive.

A lion circles close in the dark and his voice groans from the desire to taste human flesh. Or is it not a lion, but the spirit of the grandmother who died and now wants to visit her family during the hours of the night?

> My aunt turned herself into a lioness. She sought for us, as she wanted to see whether we were still comfortable where we lived . . . she, when she had smelt our houses' scent, she passed in front of us, she roared like a lioness because she wished that we should hear her, that it was she who had come seeking for us. (Dia!kwain)

Janette pointed to a single nail fixed in the ground as part of the measurements she had made on this same site some thirty years ago. She scratched at the red sand to find fragments of ash from a fire, but there were no fragments of cooked bone. She picked up little pieces of ostrich shell cut into perfect beads for a necklace and worked flints dating from the Middle Stone Age, their edges blunted by the millennia. There were also many recent flints that could have been made by //Kabbo or by his son-in-law /Hantkass'o. Janette said that when she did fieldwork here she took samples of charcoal, ostrich-egg shell, and bone fragments for radiocarbon dating, and the results all hovered around the

245

1830s: the period //Kabbo was remembering when he spoke to Wilhelm Bleek and Lucy, a time before everything was changed.

I started to examine the ground beneath my feet, my mind abstracted and distant as I picked up one stone and then another, searching for the marks of human transformation. The more I looked, the more I saw. Some of the stones that seemed to lie so casually on the surface were fixed to their chosen place as if they were being held there by deep roots.

I found a piece of worked white quartz – *!gwa-!gwara* – and as I cradled it loosely in my hand I could feel the worked sharpness of its edges, the deadly point that was once tipped with poison and bound to an arrow shaft.

In *Specimens of Bushman Folklore* /Han≠kass'o tells of the songs of the blue crane. In one of them he sings that the 'krie-boom' berries lie on his shoulders, and in another, when he is running away from a man who pursues him, he sings of the shape of his own white-feathered head, which looks like a stone arrow-head or a stone knife.

> //kurru a !kuita A splinter of stone that is white!
> //kurru a !kuita A splinter of stone that is white!
> //kurru a !kuita A splinter of stone that is white!
> (/Han≠kass'o)

Janette was looking for fragments of pottery and Elrina said she once found an almost complete pottery bowl somewhere close by. I joined in the search, but to me every brown stone looked as if it might be fired clay.

> The women pound the clay, making it soft. They pound the grass making it soft. They put the grass into the clay and they make the clay wet and they make the clay very nice and they smooth it with a piece of bone . . . they set

it down to dry in the sun. They make a little pot that is beautiful. (/Hanǂkass'o)

Above all else it was the grinding stones that held me. There were quite a few of them within the perimeter of the huts. The stones that had been chosen for this purpose were not much bigger than the span of my two hands and they were a grey colour tinged with an orangey red and I don't know their geological name. They had been cracked open with a particular skill so that the two halves remembered each other perfectly and could grind seeds, roasted locusts, anything that needed to be turned into an edible powder. But the thing about them, the thing that impressed me so much, was the energy you could see on the grinding surfaces, so that looking at them I seemed to witness the work they had done over the many years of their use. And with that this barren place sprang into life, and people like the line of people I once saw when my eyes were closed were walking towards me, and I could almost hear their voices, could almost see their faces as they gathered in this place which was their home.

> //Kabbo married, bringing !Kuobba-an to the place . . . therefore he did growing old, sit with his wife at the place while he felt that his son and his daughter did married sit. The children did speak, they did themselves feed themselves while they felt they did talk understandingly . . . They did work their houses nicely while //Kabbo's house did stand in the middle while his children did dwell on either.

And then with the same energy that brought the thought of them into being, //Kabbo and his people had gone and his people's place was nothing more than a few stones on a patch of sand.

The people's houses vanished. The wind blew away their sheltering bushes and their houses, while the people could not see on account of the dust. (/Han‡kass'o)

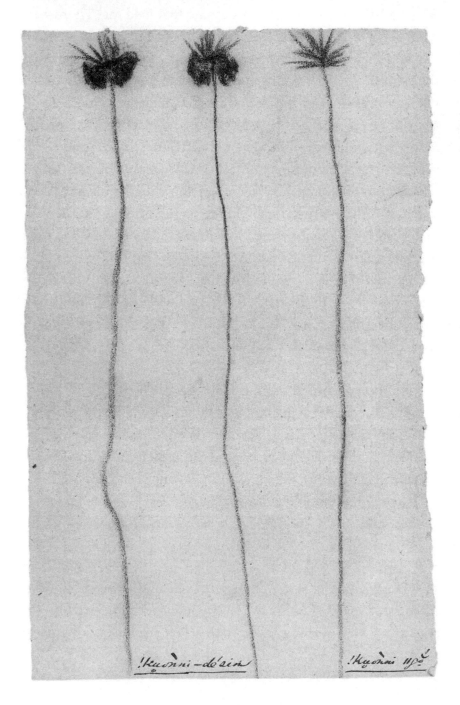

XLII

13 January 2021. A friend came round an hour ago to give me some empty jam jars for the marmalade I am about to make, so a little army of them filled to the brim with bitter sweetness can line up side by side in the cupboard as proof that the future is there, ready to be entered.

As she was leaving, my friend asked if I thought we had reached the beginning of the end of the world and we both laughed rather shyly because perhaps it might be so. Nothing to be done except boil the Seville oranges until they are soft, chop them, strain the pithy bits, add the sugar and cook and stir until something like the right moment has been reached. 'Handle a large kingdom as if you were cooking small fish,' said Lao-tzu almost three thousand years ago. 'Fortune and misfortune have no fixed abode, this one and the other are given us in turn,' said T'ao Ch'ien a thousand years later.

My friend and I did briefly wonder whether we should have a little supply of pills that would carry us away if life became too difficult, and for a while it seemed like a practical idea that could sit comfortably alongside the jars of marmalade, but then it lost its shine as it were. During childhood I learned to slip into a private world that kept me safe from whatever dangers surrounded me, and maybe that has made me mostly quite good at feeling quiet in my bones when there is trouble, if bones is where quiet is lodged. I love the people I love and I love my children and their children more than all the world and I have this book to finish and once it is finished I must face the huge task of checking the spelling of /Xam names and words, all of which need accents and breaks that cannot be found on my laptop. So here I am, where I am.

I have been thinking of the /Xam story of the ostrich feather as told by /A!kunta. It is feels like something I once knew but have since forgotten, and in that way it brings me as close as I can get to an understanding of things I do not understand.

> The man kills an ostrich. He carries the ostrich to the house. His wife takes off the short feathers that were inside the net because they are bloody. She goes to place them on the bushes. A little wind comes to them. It blows on the feather that was bloody. The wind lifts the feather into the sky. The feather falls, whirling down out of the sky. It falls into the water. It gets legs while it is still in the water. It gets feathers. It puts on wings. It sits in the sun by the water's edge because it is a young ostrich . . . He is a feather that became an ostrich when the wind blew the feather up into the air. He lets himself grow until he is grown, so that he may afterwards go to his old place, the place where he died.

I have been disentangling the three days I spent at Arbeidsvreug because they were so very tightly packed. Bitterpits in the morning of 17 March, the dwelling sites in the full heat of the sun, and in the afternoon we walked from the house to the hill called Tafelkop, or Table Hill.

This was where //Kabbo and his father and his father's father would stand in the early morning like sentinels looking down on the flat lands below, watching for the stir of movement, their arrows tipped with poison and at the ready.

They cannot ask the sun for anything but they do ask the Moon. They raise the right hand and say, 'I speak with this hand here, that I may kill springbok with my hand, with my bow. I ask that early in the morning I may kill springbok.' (/Han‡kass'o)

//Kabbo and /Han‡kass'o used to hunt ostrich together, approaching them on all fours, in the dry riverbed of the Klein Hartebees Rivier, which they called the-!Kwarra-!kwarra, and /Han‡kass'o spoke of the dry valley just south of the Tafelkop.

. . . It is the one we call //Kao. When the ostriches have slept, the ostriches awake and the ostriches assemble on it.

Maybe it was because in my own way I felt close to //Kabbo and to /Han‡kass'o that I was more acutely aware of the majesty of this hill that was their hill, the boulders scattered across it like giant glass beads that had only just stopped rolling. Some boulders had a surface that was wrinkled and pockmarked and almost sticky to look at, presumably because of the speed at which the magma had cooled under the breath of a wind, others had burst open like the jigsaw of a hatched egg. I saw one boulder with a long segment that was held in the moment when it began to split away from what you might call its parent, and if you tapped up and down the segment with a round stone it produced a reverberating succession of musical notes. I thought of Dia!kwain and the ringing sound in the sky which had now gone silent.

I do not hear the ringing in the sky which I used to hear. Therefore when I sleep, I do not feel any thing which vibrates in me when I am asleep. For when I was asleep I used to hear a thing which sounded as if a person called me.

251

Walking through the crowd of boulders I felt very contented, and when I sat down among them, the sun on my face, they were almost like companions. Each time I found a new image of an animal scratched into the glistening black rock, it was as if I was seeing the animal itself, moving somewhere close by.

On the evening of that day, we went back to the Tafelkop for a braai, not on the hill's summit, but on a flat area which could be reached in a truck. There were boulders here too, but they were less densely packed, having moved away from each other as they rolled further down the slope. They stood about and seemed to look at us, as impassive and as powerful as carved stone gods.

Elrina and her mother had brought everything that was needed: the meat, the barbecue, a few chairs, beer and ice and sticky sweet cakes called koeksisters. The sky was turning pink and apricot and the tilted sliver of the moon appeared from behind the ridge of the hill and hung among the stars.

> Mother spoke, she said, 'The moon is carrying people who are dead. You can see for yourself how it lies. It lies hollow . . . you can expect to hear something when the moon lies like this. Someone has died.' (Dia!kwain)

> !Xugen-ddi called the stars' names. He sang and called the stars' names.

Roger erected a half-kilometre-long line of fluttering red kites that rose in an arc across the sky, their silver tails glinting like flames when they were touched by the light of his torch. They looked very pretty, but for my part I would have given ten miles of fluttering kites for a little flock of birds flying over us against the tumbling apricot sun, or the silhouette of a single owl.

Roger was talking with Elrina. She and her mother were having a terrible struggle maintaining the farm and he said this landscape would make a perfect site for a game park, maybe even a game park in which the animals could just be here without any-one needing to shoot them, especially if there was also a spa and a swimming pool and natural healing, that sort of thing. She lis-tened and considered his words.

We drank beer and ate grilled lamb chops and something called skilpadges, or little tortoises, which were lumps of lambs' liver cooked in a web of fat with a curry sauce to keep them com-pany. Everything around us was poised and still. I talked with Paul in the gathering dark which makes talking easier and he spoke of the time when he was fighting apartheid and South Africa's future seemed to be on the cusp of transformation, but now a different set of bureaucrats were in charge. He spoke of his work and how he had spent some thirty years following the different Bushmen groups and photographing them, but in this present time he saw no hope of them finding a way of life that made sense within the realities of the modern world.

Who are these people here? It is /Hank um sitting there.
It is Kharru. It is !Kayo sitting. Ts'uru is standing. (//Kabbo)

I realised that none of my companions were shocked in the way that I was shocked, by the desolation of the landscape. They were able to concentrate on its qualities: the scattering of stars, the sliver of the moon in the dark sky, the looming presence of the hill and its storytelling boulders. I think that perhaps for them our human presence was enough; we were making this place mean-ingful and nothing was missing.

We gathered up the remains of our meal and drove back to the farm. Once again I lay in the bed in which Elrina's father had lain, listening to the steady breath of the wind pump while the cool air of the night poured over my face like a little stream of water. In the morning I looked at a framed collection of photo-graphs of Nak in the kitchen, and I could follow his transformation from a man who was big and strong and energetic to one who was thin and frail, with death moving close. He did not look as if he was afraid of death, or at least I could not see his fear.

Our friend is right before us . . . because he feels that he does not want to go away and leave us. The part of him with which he still thinks of us: that is what comes before us. (Dia!kwain)

XLIII

1 February 2021. I have had the vaccine. My appointment was for 5.10 and it was already growing dark when I arrived at the health centre. I found myself surrounded by something like a wartime spirit of comradery which I have never known before in England or anywhere else for that matter. Flags waving as it were, people singing jolly songs while saluting the Queen as she passed by in her golden carriage as it were.

I vaguely knew the nurse who gave me the injection and that was nice, and I enjoyed the sensation of the touch of a hand on my bare arm. And then I sat in a big room for ten minutes, my white plastic chair at a safe distance from the other white plastic chairs as if we were waiting for the start of a school exam; all of us keeping silent and still to see if we might suffer from some sort of aftershock.

When I got home and opened the door and entered my house I burst into tears. The injection seemed to have made it possible for me to realise the enormity and the danger of this time that we are in.

I have had two days of quiet as my thoughts settled, but now I am ready to return to the Karoo and the morning of the third and final day at Arbeidsvreug. We were to visit the neighbouring farmer, whose land included another range of low dolerite hills which I had seen shimmering in the distance.

My cold was not getting any better and the shame of it hemmed me in. Nobody shunned me, but they could not help looking in my direction when a cough erupted like the cry of a strange bird. We had no internet connection here where Work is Joy; nevertheless we were all aware of the virus in the wider world, lying just out of our reach, and I suppose we were all wondering what it was doing. I was reminded of the page in *Vanity Fair* in which Emily is thinking of her beloved George, while George is lying on the field of Waterloo, dead, with a bullet in his skull.

We began by driving to a farm called Nooitgedacht, which can be translated as Who'd Have Thought It. The farmer accompanied us up the hill; or perhaps he met us there, I am not sure.

Janette knew him quite well from previous visits and he was big and friendly in a way that an English landowner might be big and friendly. The label on his shorts held the word *dorpen*, alongside a cartoon image of the heads of two sheep. He told us about making a joke with his black work colleagues: he pushed them to one side in a queue and the joke's punchline was that he had forgotten apartheid was over and everyone was now equal and with that they all laughed together. He had been a lawyer until he was struck down by an illness from which he was not expected to recover, and when he did recover he gave up his work in the city and took over the running of this farm and changed its name in honour of his change of fortunes. He was inhabiting the sense of bonus time that is often given to people who have survived death, and he and his wife would sometimes drive out onto the land in the evening, and sit down on camping chairs with a bottle of good wine and a braai sizzling on the coals and he had never thought he could be so happy. He was very interested in Bushman history; their stories, their culture and their presence on the land that was now his. 'He speaks of them as if they were his, his dead children,' I wrote in my notebook but I am not quite sure what I meant by that. 'We are now in the same position as the Bushman, because of this eight-year drought,' he said.

So there we were, in the clear sunlight and in the company of more black boulders. Close to the hill's summit, Janette sat down with the farmer next to another image of the Rain Bull, whose body was slashed with the marks of a knife, the blood splattering to the ground, so that the rain would fall and the people would be able to survive.

> My mother told me, people pull out the water cow, they
> will lead her over the place, that the rain should fall on
> their places, that the onion leaves should come out. That
> they will live. If the rain does not quite fall, then they will
> die. (Dia!kwain)

She explained how a trance state can carry you to a place of transformation between the visible and the invisible world, and we all listened attentively, glancing at the Rain Bull.

We walked up to the hill's rounded summit where Who'd Have Thought It Farm reached the barbed-wire boundary dividing it from Keelafsnee – Throat Cut Farm – where someone had been murdered. There were a number of human figures cut into the boulders here: the thin outline of men with erect penises, alongside the animals with whom they lived in such intimate closeness. Someone in a previous time had scratched and hacked at these naked bodies for the sake of the idea of decency, and there was also a boulder on which in 1938, and again in 1939, a strong metal tool had been used to cover the /Xam images of trance animals with the names of two Dutchmen, followed by the carefully incised words from Psalm 50: 'And in the day of great trouble, thou shalt call upon me and I will deliver thee and thou shalt glorify my name.'

On the hill I saw a lizard, but I do not know what sort of lizard it was.

> The Agama lizard is known as the noisy rejoicer. It lies up
> on the thorn tree, it keeps its head towards the place where

the north wind blows and bewitches the rain clouds.
(/Han‡kass'o)

I also saw an odd speckled beetle that looked a bit like a spider and a meerkat skull that lay on its side, the white bone and even the teeth stained to a soft ochre colour.

Leaving Nooitgedacht I travelled back in the truck with Elrina, and as she drove, she told me more stories of her life. She said her father's father was an angry man who nicknamed her the Unnecessary One because she was born after her brother and so was nothing more than an extra mouth to feed. That same grandfather insisted he could never remember his daughter-in-law was called Alma unless he looked at the almanac hanging on the wall.

'There is a lot of my blood here,' said Elrina, as if reminded of the fact by the redness of the land. Throughout her childhood on the farm, she never had shoes strong enough to resist the sharpness of stones, the spikes on thorn bushes and the jagged remnants of metal and bone, all of it waiting to inflict their damage. Her feet would bleed from cornering a sheep or chasing a lamb that had run away, and she often had blisters as big as a fifty-pence coin; although as I write this I mistrust my own notes because surely they don't have such coins in South Africa. She would offer her battered feet to the sheep dog and he would lick the wounds and that made them heal faster. After her grandfather died, her mother gave her a first pair of good strong shoes.

She asked if I would like to come for a swim in the other water tank – I call it tank number 2 in my notes. And so instead of going straight back to the house we drove on until we reached another incongruous construction standing all on its own in the middle of this nowhere. It was built from concrete blocks and the inside was lined with some sort of rubberised canvas. To get in one had to climb onto an old chair left there for the purpose and then it was quite easy to plop over the edge into the green and slightly salty water. I went first as the honoured guest, wearing knickers and a bra, and the water was up to my waist, while my feet wondered what on earth they might be standing on. I swam around in small circles for a while, feeling my body relaxing after so much sun and wind and the concentration of looking for things I did not know how to recognise. Elrina went in after I had got out and I dried myself on the white T-shirt that was supposed to have special qualities to reflect the sun's rays, but was not much good as a towel.

> The water will flow into the water pits and into the pans.
> It will lie in them. It will fill them up. Then the springbok shall go along and drink . . . The ostriches will go to wash their flesh.

The more Elrina and I talked, the more close I felt to a shared sense of the isolation of our childhoods and presumably of her father's childhood as well; both of them finding comfort and companionship from the thought of the /Xam who had lived here and who seemed to watch over them in a more benevolent way than old Jehovah with his righteous anger.

!kau:xu: hunting ground
!kau: to live, to be alive
!k'au: earth, dust ground
:xu: face, surface, head

She pointed out a plastic water pipe leading from the tank that had been chewed by a porcupine, and said she could not understand why it would choose to eat something so inedible and she had better come back later and set a trap for it. I hoped she did not mean to shoot the porcupine, and she assured me she would release it on the other side of the fence. I have only once seen a porcupine in the wild; the heavy head hung down as if from shyness and the black glimmer of its eye glanced at me to see if I meant to do harm, and now my heart was racing with fear for the life of this one that I had not seen.

When these Stars have turned back, the porcupine will not remain on the hunting ground, for he knows that it is dawn . . . He returns home, for he is used to looking at these Stars and he feels that he knows they are the dawn's Stars. (/Han‡kass'o)

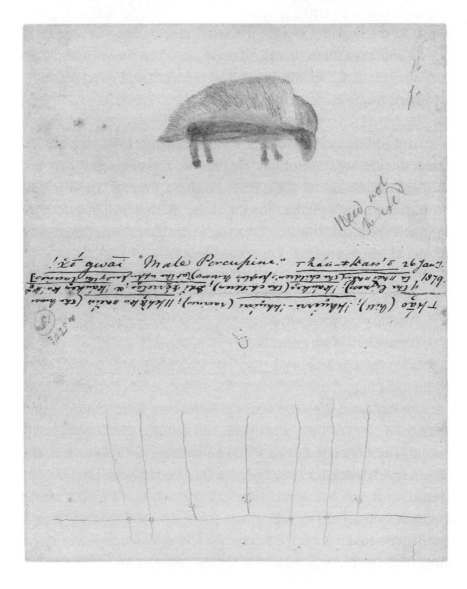

Elrina said she liked to hunt and she would kill an animal in a trap if she felt it was necessary, but unlike her brother and her grandfather, she would never kill for fun. I must have asked what she meant by necessary, because she told me that jackals still get onto the land in spite of the fences and she had to kill them whenever she could, and the equally determined wild cats known as caracals had to go as well, which was a pity because they were so beautiful. As if to illustrate the necessity of the act of killing and also the savagery of it, she told me how, as a young child, eight years old or even less, her father had trapped and shot a female caracal and showed her where the babies were, huddled in fear within the animal's lair. Without pausing to think of the act, but perhaps wanting to impress her father and the other members of her family who had gathered around, the little girl picked up one and then another of these babies and dashed their brains out against the side of the truck.

> We sleep soundly in the bushes' inside shade which is cool. The dog drags us out and we wake screaming out of sleep. We are frightened to die, frightened that we are almost dead . . . the man is holding a stick and the dog is biting us and dragging us out from our little house. The dog, biting us, will lay us flat upon the ground and the dog's man will beat our heads while we lie on the ground . . . We call to our companions, so they must run away when they hear us screaming loudly. The other jackals think that death is with us and so they run out of the shade. (//Kabbo)

Turning back again to her childhood, Elrina told me how she was given a springbok kid as a pet, presumably because the parent had been shot. It was beautiful and elegant and would come to her when she called, but I forgot to ask if she gave it a name. For some time it lived quite contentedly with the sheep, but then something happened, I suppose it must have crossed over into adulthood, and with that it recognised the sheep as strangers, but anyway it began to attack them with its horns, jabbing at their fat tails and ripping at their stomachs. And so the springbok had to die.

> And we slept at home and the springbok that night came to sleep at the place at which we had buried my wife. These things are those which we shall not speak of, we will remain silent. (Dia!kwain)

Elrina attributed a wanton violence to many of the wild animals she spoke of. The porcupine unnecessarily eating the plastic pipe, the springbok damaging the surface of the veld with their sharp feet, the cruelty of jackals and hyenas. I must have asked why some native species could not be allowed to live within the confines of the farm, but it was clearly a foolish question; there was only so much grass, so much water, and everything else followed as surely as night follows day. She said there had been no springbok here since the late 1970s, no kudu, no eland, no ostrich for a long time and of course no elephants. As if to quieten my disquiet, she told me that some farmers turned their land into game parks, which meant that, instead of sheep, a certain number of wild animals were bought and released within the fenced areas so that tourists could pay to come and kill them.

And yet, and yet, and yet, this is a good and gentle woman who has needed to adapt and survive in the place which she loves above all else, and I don't think she has seen much in the way of choice, and maybe if I had been her I would have come to the same conclusions. And so we drove back to the farm and to another friendly supper.

XLIV

7 February 2021. I now only have a single guinea pig because the two brothers rose up against each other, long incisor teeth bared in their curiously narrow mouths, and they slashed and bit and one of them was almost blinded by a wound above the eye which clouded over with a milky film. I washed it with salty water that was no stronger than tears and the eye recovered and I gave the aggressor to three little girls who came to collect it with their father and a collecting box and I have kept the victim. Every morning I bring him into the kitchen for a couple of hours and he sits on the counter on top of the fridge and eats lettuce leaves, cabbage leaves, perhaps a slice of red pepper. Having eaten, he goes to sleep, sitting on a dishcloth, his head nodding. I exhort him to be more friendly but he does not listen. Guinea pigs are not good listeners although they can be quite conversational.

The idea of the lockdown has turned into the physical reality of being locked down because for the last few days we have been cut off by heavy falls of snow. It began with a strong wind swooping the snow into drifts and sculpted heaps and now the wind has been replaced by stillness and everything is transformed by the shock of whiteness. Within the silence I think of my children and grandchildren, the excited laughter as they play together and I join in and play with them.

On that final day at Arbeidsvreug, we all went to watch the 120 sheep being rounded up by Elrina's neighbour who was in charge of them, now that she and her mother were not able to spend much time here.

We again drove a bit of a distance until we reached a pen made out of gates and bits of fencing, into which the sheep were to be driven and then dipped against whatever it was they needed to be protected from. I don't remember the farmer's face, just the solid build of his body, and the way he stood with feet firmly planted on the ground, his wide thick shoulders and a sort of mechanical stiffness of movement.

The sheep were being rounded up by four or five thin men riding on motorbikes – I wonder now if they were quad bikes, but I don't think so because I can see them leaning over towards the ground as they took one fast sharp turn and then another, skidding and swerving as if they were in a race against each other.

The sheep began to arrive. All but a few of them had black faces and white cropped fleeces stained by dust and sand. They looked rough and skinny and terrified, and it was as if they had never met humans before and had never been chased like this and they were running for their lives, skidding and swerving and desperate, their eyes in a mad wide stare of panic.

The bulk of the flock was quickly funnelled into the pen, but a few stragglers had broken away and they were pursued by the men on motorbikes who swerved after them through the obstacle race of low bushes. The farmer stood and watched. We stood and watched. Finally all these strange ungainly creatures had been gathered and they were cowering in the corner of the pen. The farmer and Elrina did a head count and then one by one they were herded into a narrow corridor of fences that took them through the dip and out into the freedom of the Karoo, to wander off looking for whatever they could find to eat on this dry land.

I used to watch the shepherd in that steep valley in North

Wales – the one who recited the poem about the people who were attacked and poisoned – bringing his sheep down from the mountains. He worked with three or four dogs, whistling soft instructions to them as they ran and leapt and moved as fast as shadows, curving around the sheep, now cutting them off, now driving them forward. The sheep often looked nonplussed and sometimes they doubled back on their tracks, trying to escape, but there was none of the blind terror I was seeing now. I once woke early in the house where I used to stay and the dogs were out on the hill on their own, the old red-coated bitch teaching her puppies to work the sheep this way and that without the need to listen to any instructions.

Or I think of the shepherd near where I often go in the mountains of Italy, and one night when the moon was full my husband and I were sitting with him, talking and eating the pasta he had cooked over an open fire, and all his sheep with their long and serious faces gathered together, impatient for him to come and milk them. And when he finally got up and went to sit in the gap in the wall with his bucket ready to be filled, they were already lined up in their usual sequence they always used and he addressed each one by name.

This lot were a ramshackle bunch, and even though they didn't have much meat on their bones, they were only kept for their meat and so there was no need to ensure that the ewes kept calm during milking, no need to watch over the lambs. They were simply strangers in a strange land and the sun blazed down on them by day, and the cold moon frightened them by night. They appeared to be such ungainly creatures, so unsuited to this environment as they slipped and skidded on the hard ground. They stood and panted, and had none of that extraordinary beauty of the springbok, the kudu, and all the other members of the antelope family that belonged here by right. They could not leap like a springbok leaps, catapulting itself into the air with a twist of pure energy, they could not defend themselves with sharp horns like a kudu or gallop at speed like an eland. Their skin was easily wounded by thorn bushes and sharp stones damaged their feet. They were too hot when they carried their coats of wool and too delicate when they were shorn, and they had no camouflage, so if jackals or caracals managed to find a way in through the fences, then they could offer no resistance to being killed and devoured – for we like sheep have gone astray.

I tried to imagine //Kabbo and all the others, witnessing the arrival of these unfamiliar beasts and the way they spread across the land to which they were always unsuited, listening to the monotonous sound of them crying in the wilderness.

Mama used to eat springbok, for mama did not possess sheep, goats or cattle. She had no flocks, but only spring-bok. (Dia!kwain)

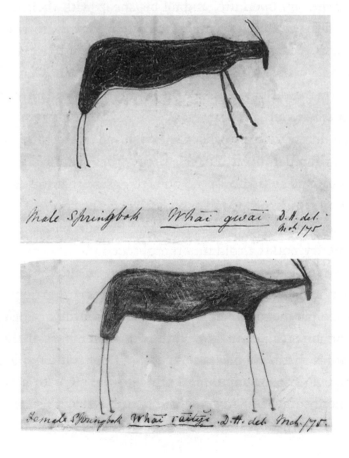

And yet it was for the sake of the sheep, that everything else had to be removed, not only the predators, but also the other eaters of the sparse food of the veld.

> They seek to feed the children . . . therefore you must talk nicely to the people when they are lying in wait for the ostrich, that the ostrich may walk up to them, that they may kill the ostrich, that they may give their children food . . . But now they do not possess ostriches. (Dia!kwain)

And once everything that might threaten the survival of the sheep had been removed, then the sheep were all that was left. //Kabbo called them 'starvation's food'.

The Bushmen were landless and as /Han‡kass'o had said to Lucy, 'there are two farmers only in his part of the country who are good to the Bushmen and who do not drive them away from the water.'

All they could do in order to live was to work as shepherds for the Boers. /Han‡kass'o described the two sorts of sheep: the ones that have fat tails will return home and the ones that do not have fat tails do not return home, but remain where they are left, standing in a flat place. He told of the strychnine and other poisons that were used to kill all predators, and he explained that even if the Bushmen worked, *they feel that they are poor people.* As food they might be given sheep fat, poured into a bowl made from the shell of a tortoise and then they could perhaps dip something into it. The meat from a dead dog was very dry, he said, but it tasted better if it was dipped in fat.

Nearly all the prisoners held at the Breakwater Jail were being punished for stealing or killing or eating a sheep and many more were murdered at the place where the crime was said to have been committed. The evidence against Dia!kwain was a sheep's skeleton, found some four miles from where he and his people were living, and that must have echoed with his childhood dream in which he and his father were cutting up a sheep and the Boer came and said 'he would beat us to death. And the dream spoke to me that I told the Boer not to kill us, but to let us work for him instead.'

The woman called Doortje was beaten on the veld by her master, because her master thought she had taken away the sheep. 'She did not know the sheep, for the sheep they were not few. The sheep were many.'

The man called Mansee was running after the sheep. 'He caught his foot. He fell down. A stone cut his knee. Therefore they called his name !Kaulnoan, Stone Knee.'

When //Kabbo left Mowbray with the hope of returning to the Bitterpits and the Tafelkop hill, he ended up living where his wife was living and working for a Boer on a sheep farm. /Han‡kass'o might have also worked on a farm, but there is no way of knowing, and ‡Kasin also disappeared without trace. Dia!kwain tried that life but could not manage it and so he set off, looking for the family he had lost, and that was when he was murdered.

The sheep scatter out across the Karoo and we go back for one last night as guests on a farm called Joy of Work.

XLV

14 February 2021. The snow remains and where it has been trodden down it has taken on a thick skin of ice. I need to be careful not to fall; it would be unwise to fall in this silent time. The chickens stay in their house, sometimes peering out with a look of dismay. There is much waiting to be done. I woke this morning with a few lines of a poem by Theodore Roethke in my head.

> This shaking keeps me steady. I should know.
> What falls away is always. And is near.
> I wake to sleep, and take my waking slow.
> I learn by going where I have to go.

It's almost a year now since we had a last breakfast in the Arbeitsvreug farmhouse and I said goodbye to Elrina and to Alma. As I left I looked once again at the photographs of Nak, father and husband, the stages of his life gathered together in a picture frame that hung on the kitchen wall close to the front door so that you met him each time you walked in or walked out. I wondered if I would ever be here again. The wind pump. The sunsets and the rising of the moon. The hard ground underfoot. The little bushes. The rounded hill in the distance. The silence by day and by night. The way the dead and the living can rub shoulders with each other.

We bundled all our things into Janette's Toyota and set off, opening and closing the farm gates and heading towards the Strandberg hills of /A!kunta and /Han‡kass'o's childhoods. I sat in the front seat staring at the land as it rolled out in front of me and I felt myself floating off, abandoning the present moment and somehow not able to return to it. I had seen enough of what was and what might have been and my mind seemed to be filled to the brim.

The Strandberg hills were much higher than the Tafelkop, their austere presences rising up like mirages from the platform of the land. Janette had arranged for the farmer who owned this area to leave a gate unlocked for us, so that we could drive up a track to the foot of the main hill and then spend much of the day there, walking about and looking at more storytelling boulders. But the farmer had taken his dog to the vet and had forgotten to open the gate, and so after trying other gates further down the road that were also locked, we continued on our journey. Later I told myself that /A!kunta, whose name meant cannot come in, must have shut the gate for me so that I could get home to my family.

A long straight road watched over by the hills. Lines of fences following us in a metallic blur and occasionally a few sheep bearing witness to our passing. And then suddenly my iPhone woke from its long sleep and started to make a succession of loud pinging noises like a hungry bird. There were numerous messages from my children, 'Mum, where are you?' 'Mum, you've got to come home!' 'Mum, give us a call!' 'Mum, there's going to be a lockdown in two days!' 'Mum, you must hurry or you won't be able to get back!' I felt suddenly dizzy from the lack of connection with everything that was familiar to me, and I think that if I had been standing, I would have fallen down.

By now we had reached the edge of a town called Vanwyksvlei, little bungalows close by and the fragile and poverty-stricken houses of a township in the distance. Janette stopped at the side of the road, next to a faded concrete sign dating from 1898 and painted with the almost but not quite illegible name of the place, surrounded by vague blobs of landscape done in soft greens and yellows. Within minutes a crowd of ragged children had gathered at a safe distance from our vehicle, hands outstretched and the now familiar whispered cry of 'hungry, hungry, hungry'.

I needed to buy a new plane ticket as quickly as possible but I was shaking too much to hold the phone. Paul took it from me and found the last but one flight to London and the last but one seat, and I had just enough presence of mind to read out the details of my bank card number to confirm the sale.

We continued on our way. I thought we were heading straight back, but Janette was determined that we should complete a bit more of our broken itinerary with a visit to the last and possibly the most beautiful of the /Xam sites: a place called Springbokoog, Springbok Eye.

And so we turned onto a rough track which eventually led us into a sort of paradise: a pool of water flanked by rushes, a variety of trees and grasses on all sides. The man who owned the land was away on business, but he had given Janette permission to visit in his absence. If I understood it right, he planned to turn the area into a game park, or perhaps a spa. There would also need to be a helicopter landing pad because you couldn't expect people to come all this way by road and no one would want to stay here for more than a few days.

We reached the foot of a more familiarly barren hill and began to walk up its side. I saw several beautiful elephants marching across one boulder and I remembered how ǂKasin had thought they were mythical creatures. I saw a racing group of eland on another boulder, their bodies straining with effort as they ran. I wondered if they were being hunted in order to summon up the rain that would bring life to the dry ground.

A man, I do not know his name, but he was one of the First at Sitting People and he once hunted the Rain, as the Rain was grazing there, for the Rain was like an eland. His breath

271

filling the flats and the hills with a mist, you could smell him coming. (Dia!kwain)

And then here were two or maybe it was three boulders which showed the elephant shrew, a mouse-like creature with a square head and a wavering trunk of a nose, and, as I have since learned, it does have a genetic connection with the elephant. The shrews on the boulder were as big as my spread hand and they looked like magical creatures that had been caught in the act of transforming between something of this world and something of the other. They seemed both huge and tiny, earthly beings that were as insubstantial as the inhabitants of a dream.

We all walked in different directions and sat and stared and walked and sat again. I took photographs of the elephant, the eland and the shrews, and photographs of the figure of a man who was lying on his back and shooting an arrow into an eland, which seemed to be acquiescing to its own death, as if the two of them had made a pact together.

> The man who has shot the eland, speaks and tells the old men about it. He does not speak loud. He speaks as if he were in pain. He quietly speaks to them. He begs them to look into the quiver to see what he has shot by the hairs on the arrow's shank. They see it is an eland which the man has shot. (/Han‡kass'o)

There was an equally intimate scene of a man standing in front of an ostrich that appeared to be holding still while he shot an arrow up into its breast.

I took a photograph of an egg-shaped ochre-coloured stone that seemed to have imploded where it lay embedded in the red sand, I suppose in response to the steady heat of the sun over more years than could be counted; the jigsaw puzzle of the moment of its disintegration tightly held. Other men and other animals were scattered among the boulders. It was a very crowded place.

And then we were off. We had booked to stay the night in a self-catering house that belonged to a woman called Rina, but when Janette stopped at the house and spoke to the woman, she did not want us because of the virus and so we drove on. We had another flat tyre. We passed the hill on which stood the column of rock that Dia!kwain said was the Young Man turned to Stone by the Glance of a New Maiden, but the Boers called Lot's Wife. Whatever its name, the rock looked like a giant human figure on the skyline. I had read several accounts of how the gaze of a maiden can steal all movement from a young man and that is why she must be taken to a special house by the old women and confined there until she ceased to be dangerous. The young man could be turned into stone, but he could also be turned into a tree.

The man climbs the mountain. He plays the goura ... The girl looks at him as he comes ... He carried the arrow. He held the bow. He was holding a jackal's tail hair. The girl looked at him and it is so that he stands and it is so that he stands still, as he holds the jackal's tail hair, standing still, holding his bow. And it is so that he became a tree, as he stood, as he held the hair.

He is a tree. He stands. He has his legs, he has his feet, he wears shoes made from the skin of the gemsbok, he is a man. He was a man, he becomes a tree because the girl looks at him with her eye, she looks, fastening him to the ground and it is so. His legs are those of a man, he is a tree. His arms are those of a man, he holds the goura with his mouth, he is a tree.

He is a man, he is a tree. He is a speaking tree which spoke standing, for he was a man. The girl looked at him and so it was that he became a tree. (//Kabbo)

We stopped at some sort of hotel to see if they would have us for the night, but they also did not want us for fear of the virus. Janette was curiously unruffled even though it would take us at least another twelve hours if we had to drive all the way to Cape Town. Then Paul remembered a friend who had a holiday house that was surely somewhere nearby. He phoned and asked if we could be her guests in her absence. He assured her that we were all healthy and I managed to restrain my cough as he spoke. The woman was not sure if it was a good idea, but she agreed on condition that we left no trace of our passing. She said she would arrange for someone to come the following day to clean all the rooms in our wake.

With the night approaching we arrived in a little town that was like a film set from another era. The streets were lined with rows of elegant nineteenth-century houses that appeared perfect in their every detail. We had arranged to collect the key from a man who lived in the town and we waited in the Toyota until he came out to meet us. He seemed afraid and nervous to the point of being angry with the task that had been given to him.

We found the house and went inside. The walls were just as they must have been when they were first plastered and papered with pale patterned wallpaper; even the paintwork on the window frames and the wainscoting looked as if it had never been altered. The table, the lampshades, the chairs, the rugs, the vases, the low china sink in the kitchen and the plates in the wooden rack, everything belonged within another time. The single black metal-framed bed in the room in which I was to sleep was made up with thick white sheets that must have been starched and ironed by hand.

We sat down in the kitchen to eat the food that Elrina had packed for us as one last gesture of her kindness, and we each had a little glass of aquavit from what was left in a bottle that Roger was carrying in his rucksack. I spoke to my daughter on the phone and told her I was flying home the next day and I heard the relief in her voice. I spoke to my son and asked him if he could collect me from the airport, but then realised that of course he could not. Before going to bed we went and stood in a paved garden surrounded by a high wall with a stable at the far end that I could almost believe was still occupied by a horse and a cart.

I slept in the little room as if I was someone other than myself. In the morning I made the bed as neat and tight as I could and picked up the heap of paper handkerchiefs that bore witness to a fit of sneezing. We all worked together to remove every trace of having been here and then drove to the house of the stranger who had given us the key and dropped it through his letter box – or did he come to the door, as if he was crouched behind it and waiting? Dawn was breaking as we set off. I worried that I might have left a paper handkerchief behind, as evidence of the sin of my contagion.

We had many hours of travel from which I remember only two things. As we were getting closer to our destination on wide, smooth, well-made roads, we began to descend into a lush valley where I was told the best South African wine is made. The land once belonged to the Khoekhoe and to their herds of big-horned cattle, but they lost it after a bitter struggle with the Boers. One of my companions said that the people who worked the grapes were paid not in money but in tots of wine that kept them in a state of permanent drunkenness.

And then, at some stage of the journey, either before or after the valley, we stopped at a petrol station and got out of the Toyota to stretch our legs. I stood in the warmth of the sunshine. A big open-topped lorry was parked close by and it was carrying live ostriches. I could see their necks swaying and twisting as if they were trying to escape from the bodies that held them, and I could see their round staring eyes, their beaks gaping with fear.

The ostrich comes out of the west when the sun is warm, when it comes to eat from ǂkeǁhann, the flower of the great thorn tree. It comes forward in the sun. It looks around, for its neck is always long, for its eyes do sit above and its eyes look far off, through the hollow of the bone. (//Kabbo)

XLVI

19 March 2021 and I have started a new vegetable bed, a narrow strip that should be big enough for a row of ten potato plants, and as I was cutting out small chunks of turf and struggling to dig into the soil that lay beneath, packed tight with a dense mesh of tree roots and stones and bits of brick, I came across a surprising number of sleepy worms and thought of Charles Darwin who made a study of the earthworm as he moved towards the final chapter of his life.

Time is coming full circle because today it is a year since I left South Africa. We reached Janette's house late in the afternoon and her brother took a photograph of the four of us looking vaguely triumphant as we stood in a line in front of the Toyota. Roger and I clambered into Paul's battered jeep and I was delivered to Tanya's house, where she and the dogs welcomed me like an old friend.

I packed my suitcase in a daze of urgency, discarding the walking boots in favour of the abalone shell and abandoning the rucksack I had bought in the market, even though it could easily be folded into a tiny bundle of thin nylon. A heap of notebooks, the hardback one big enough to hold the painting of the line of people walking towards me safe between its pages. Photocopies, but none of the drawings by Dia!kwain and /Han‡kass'o and the four !Kun children that are presumably still waiting for me to collect them. A couple of new books. The remains of the propolis. Two small stones, their colours holding a recollection of //Kabbo's place. No ostrich egg, even though I often imagine it being here on top of the bookcase, ready to be used in case I wanted to 'drink at the house of water'. Two pairs of socks from the market, an L and an R written into their pattern so I would always know which one belonged to which foot; the luminous T-shirt, the pale trousers, the skirt, the knickers, the little green tin of Xam-Buk lip balm, a bunch of driedoring twigs, the pale leaves already crumbling into dust.

Tanya drove me to the airport. We passed the road that led towards the Company's Gardens with its pigeons and bronze men on plinths, and then we were on the motorway and there was the turning to what had been the little village of Mowbray on our left while the overcrowded township was stretched out on our right. And then suddenly and almost imperceptibly I was on my own, queuing up at a desk with my passport ready to be presented and my face partially covered by the snout-like white mask my friend Jayne had given me as a precaution before I left for Cape Town.

The airport lounge was almost empty, probably because there was only the one flight setting off that evening. I bought a packet of rooibos tea and some biltong, those sticks of dried meat. I wanted to buy a fridge magnet made of tin, showing the side of a rather fat airplane filled with happy smiling travellers who gazed out from the windows, but although I had a bundle of green paper notes, I did not have enough of them.

And then I was on the crowded plane and the man who was losing his mind was leaning his mind-losing head on my shoulder and the man with the fever was fidgeting in the seat in front of me. I watched a film about a woman with snaggled teeth and roughly dyed hair who lived with her mother in a little stone dwelling somewhere in Eastern Europe and she kept bees in a crack in a cliff and more bees in the hollow trunk of a tree. A travelling family came and cut down the tree to get at the honey, but the bees in the cliff were safe and I entered a fitful sleep and woke as the dawn was filling the sky.

> //Kabbo is the one who thinks of the place, //Kabbo must be the one to return to the place. He waits for the return of the moon, that he may return.
>
> I sit waiting for the moon to turn its back for me, that I may set my feet on the path, that I may return to my place. That I may listen to all the people's stories when I visit them, while the sun becomes a little warm, that I might sit in the sun, that I might sit listening to the stories that come from afar, while the sun feels a little warm, while I feel that I might be talking with my fellow men.

As I watch myself stepping out into the arrivals hall, pulling the black suitcase on wheels behind me, I am reminded of a video installation I once saw with my husband. As you approached you heard the sound of monks chanting, the rise and fall of their voices like waves beating against a shore, and on the wall at the far end of an alcove the video playing in an endless loop of repetition. It showed the arrivals hall in an unidentified airport, and as the big glass sliding doors opened and closed, one person and then another emerged from the limbo of travel and into the reality of a different country. The film had been slowed right down so that as the people moved they seemed to be caught in a trance of apprehension. There was a terrible sadness in the way they turned their heads this way and that to see if anyone had come to welcome them, to embrace them, to make them feel they belonged.

> My fellow men are those who are listening to stories from other places, stories which float along. I must sit cooling my arms that the tiredness may go from them, because I sit. I listen, watching for a story which I want to hear while

I sit waiting for it that it may float into my ear. I sit silent, while I listen along the road, while I feel that my name floats along the road, that my three names float along to my place.

So there I was on the morning of 20 March 2020, stepping through sliding doors and hoping to see a familiar face among the gathered crowd of strangers, even though I knew there would be no one waiting for me apart from a taxi driver who held up my name written in capital letters on a piece of paper. He was courteous, Turkish, a student. He also wore a mask. He drove me home. I thanked him. Friends had left a box of food outside the locked door of my house.

I must go together with the warm sun, while the earth is warm. A little path it is not, for a great path it is. The path is long. I must go to my place when the trees are dry. For I shall walk while the flowers become dry, while I go along, keeping to the path and then autumn will quickly come upon me while I sit at my place, for I will not go to places which are different, for I must stay at my place.

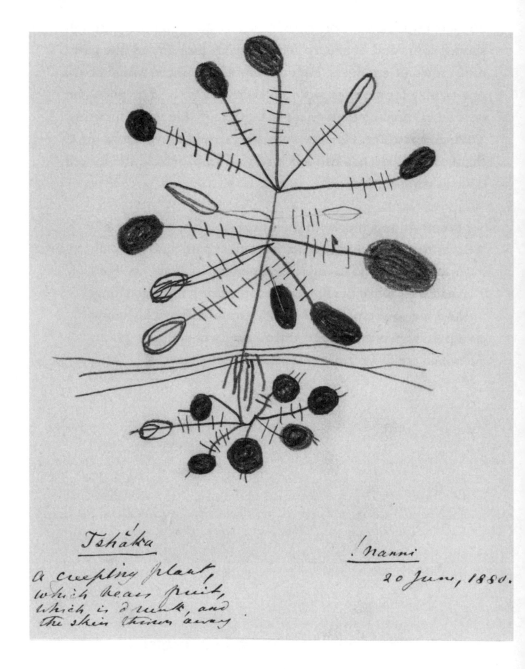

Tsháku

A creeping plant,
which bears fruit,
which is drunk, and
the skin thrown away

!nanni

20 June, 1880.

Postscript

On 18 April 2021 a wildfire that had been raging in the Table Mountain National Park entered the University of Cape Town campus. The reading room of the Jagger Library, which holds one of the most prestigious and crucial archive collections for South Africa's history, was terribly damaged, and much of its African Studies Collection of some sixty-five thousand books, twenty-six thousand pamphlets, three thousand African films and twenty thousand audio visual items were destroyed.

It was feared that the entire Bleek-Lloyd Archive might have also been lost in the flames, but luckily it was stored in the basement and the fire doors functioned well.

Select Bibliography

Books and Publications

Andrew Bank, *Bushmen in a Victorian World: The remarkable story of the Bleek – Lloyd Collection of Bushman folklore* (Double Storey Books, Cape Town, 2006).

Neil Bennun, *The Broken String: The Last Words of an Extinct People* (Viking Penguin, London, 2004).

Morgan Bisele, *Women Like Meat: The Folklore and Foraging Ideology of the Kalahari Ju/'hoan* (Witwatersrand University Press, Johannesburg, 1993).

W. H. I. Bleek & L. C. Lloyd, *Specimens of Bushman Folklore* (George Allen, London, 1911).

Hugh Brody, *The Other Side of Eden: Hunter-Gatherers, Farmers and the Shaping of the World* (Faber & Faber, London, 2001).

H. J. Deacon & Janette Deacon, *Human Beginnings in South Africa: Uncovering the Secrets of the Stone Age* (David Philip Publishers, Cape Town and Johannesburg, 1999).

Janette Deacon, ' "My Place is the Bitterpits": the home Territory of Bleek and Lloyd's /Xam San Informants', *African Studies*, 45 (2), 1986.

Janette Deacon, 'Insights into the /Xam Universe Before the Ska' (unpublished article, 2017).

Janette Deacon and Thomas A. Dowson (eds), *Voices from the Past: /Xam Bushmen and the Bleek and Lloyd Collection* (Witwatersrand University Press, Johannesburg, 1996).

Jared Diamond, *Guns, Germs and Steel* (Vintage, London, 1998).

Sandy Gall, *The Bushmen of Southern Africa* (Chatto & Windus, London, 2001).

V. G. Kiernan, *The Lords of Human Kind: European Attitudes to the Outside World in the Imperial Age* (Weidenfeld & Nicolson, London, 1969).

Sven Lindqvist, *Exterminate All the Brutes* (Granta, London, 1997).

Mark McGranaghan, *Foragers on the frontiers: the /Xam Bushmen of the North-ern Cape, South Africa, in the nineteenth century*, DPhil thesis, University of Oxford (2012) (https://ora.ox.ac.uk/objects/uuid:5d935fc4-648d-427b-8ac0-c134c1e3e755).

Elizabeth Marshall Thomas, *The Harmless People* (Knopf, New York, 1958).

David Olusoga & Casper W. Erichsen, *The Kaiser's Holocaust: Germany's Forgot-ten Genocide and the Colonial Roots of Nazism* (Faber & Faber, London, 2010).

José Manuel de Prada-Samper (recorder and ed.), *The Man Who Cursed the Wind and other stories from the Karoo* (African Sun Press in association with the Centre for African Studies, University of Cape Town Press, 2016).

Pippa Skotnes (ed.), *Miscast* (University of Cape Town Press, 1996).

Pippa Skotnes (ed.), *Claim to the Country: The Archive of Wilhelm Bleek and Lucy Lloyd* (Jacanna, Johannesburg and Cape Town, 2008).

J. C. Smuts, *Jan Christian Smuts: A Biography* (Cassell, 1952).

Marlene Winberg, *Annotations of Loss and Abundance: An examination of the !kun children's material in the Bleek and Lloyd Collection (1879–1881)* (University of Cape Town Press, 2011).

Archives

Bleek and Lloyd Archive, housed at the University of Cape Town, the National Library and Iziko South African Museum. The archive can be accessed online at http://lloydbleekcollection.cs.uct.ac.za/. Lucy Lloyd's Notebooks, housed at the Jagger Library, University of Cape Town.

Notes

44   *Grandfather turned himself*: Archive, 5069.

44   *He is a lion*: Ibid., 277–8.

45   *The lion says*: Ibid., 1167.

45   *It seemed as if*: Ibid., 5866.

45   *When the people see*: Bennun, p. 211.

45   *I resemble my father*: Archive, 733–9.

45   *The baboon is*: Ibid., 7296–8.

46   *We shall see*: Ibid., 5553–4.

47   *A presentiment is*: Bleek & Lloyd, pp. 331–9.

47   *We feel in our*: Archive, 2532.

48   *He feels the rustling*: Ibid., 2554–6.

50   *Oh old woman!*: Bank, p. 273.

53   *Darkness resembles fear*: Archive, 373.

54   *I shall drink*: Bank, p. 36.

54   *!gam ke ǂei*: Ibid., p. 39.

54   *Koi-ang is the*: Archive, 189.

55   *There is my wife*: Bleek & Lloyd, pp. 291–9.

56   *The doctor asked*: The entire story of //Kabbo's capture and journey to Cape Town is in Bleek & Lloyd, pp. 291–9.

57   *We came to Beaufort*: Bennun, pp. 22–4.

60   a film called *Tracks*: Hugh Brody, *Tracks across Sand*, 2012.

64   *Khou/khougen*: Archive, 1130.

66   a documentary: John Marshall, *A Kalahari Family*, 2002.

71   *The Bushmen hold*: Archive, 1261.

72   *Mother beat the ground*: Ibid., 4803–5.

74   *Where else shall*: Charles White, *An Account of the Regular Graduations in Man*, 1799.

74   *Yet, if we wield*: Charles Lyell, *Principles of Geology*, 1830–33.

74   *There must be a physical*: Robert Knox, *The Races of Men*, London, 1850.

74   *They are without a past*: Frederick Farrar, 'Aptitude of the Races', lecture to the Ethnological Society of London, 1866.

74   *there is no longer room*: George McCall Theal, *The Yellow and Dark-Skinned People of Africa South of the Zambesi*, Swan Sonnenschein & Co., 1911.

75   In 1854 Bleek: This account of Bleek's early life is from Bennun, p. 81.

76   *A German, Dr Bleek*: Ibid., p. 101.

77   *her private parts*: Bank, p. 37.

78   *One of my wife's sisters*: Bennun, p. 72.

80   *The moon comes out*: Archive, 292–3.

82   *because its apparently primitive*: quoted in Bank, p. 71.

84   *The water shall rain*: Archive, 2047.

84   *Give bread*: quoted in Bennun, p. 40.

85   *the valuable assistance . . . gratefully acknowledged the help*: Ibid., pp. 278, 272.

86   *thu: white man*: Archive, 373–4.

87   *a brush called /ku*: Ibid., 1121–2.

88   *As he is knocking*: Ibid., 938.

89   *The old woman*: Ibid., 2160.

93   *The cat, the wild cat*: Ibid., Jantje at the Museum, 30 May 1871.

94   *When a man kills*: quoted in Bennun, p. 233.

94   *The people eat ostriches*: Archive, 458.

98   *I must eat*: Ibid., 1141–4.

98   *My thoughts spoke*: Bennun, p. 7.

98   *The Bushman dies*: Archive, 1173.

98   *A man leaves*: Ibid., 1217–329.

101 *In the past*: Ibid., 6709–10.

103 *My mother was*: Ibid., 2510–15.

103 *The dawn did not*: Ibid., 2211.

103 *Our mothers told me*: Ibid., 594–7, 5776.

103 *The people dying*: Ibid., 1426–30.

104 *The old pot*: Ibid., 7316–19.

105 *The things that are*: Ibid., 5788–90.

107 *//Kabbo was the second*: Ibid., 476.

107 *I saw them*: Ibid., 1949–51.

108 *She did say*: Ibid., 1953–6.

109 *He has feet*: Ibid., 306.

110 *I must possess*: Bleek & Lloyd, pp. 299–317.

110 *The mountains lie*: Archive, 1357–73.

114 *His mother is said*: Ibid., 2414.

114 *The Boers bound them*: Bennun, p. 222.

114 *Hwurri-terri who was*: Archive, 5872–80.

116 *I smear the poison*: Ibid., 3476–80.

117 */hunn-ta-Oho: a piece of root*: Ibid., 3425–3.

118 *The honeybees*: Ibid., 1364–6.

121 *The men all lay dead*: Archive, 2483–6.

122 *The place became*: Ibid., 5104–9.

123 *just as if*: Bennun, pp. 259–61; Archive, 5110–16.

124 *Mother did not know*: Archive, 5139–40.

125 *At the time*: Ibid., 5199.

125–6 Bank, pp. 256–61, and Bennun, pp. 266–72.

126 *Grandfather !Nwin/kuiten*: Archive, 5101.

126 *the cultural intellect*: quoted in Bank, p. 257.

127   *When the moon*: Bleek & Lloyd, p. 399.

128   *Mother took a stone*: Archive, 5160–2.

128   *Why can it be*: quoted in Bank, pp. 262–3.

129   *When the sun*: Archive, 4684.

130   *Bushmen who lived*: Grey Library, Cape Town, 28 February 1878, UCT C15.14.

131   *An owl made*: Archive, 4868.

135   *We clap our hands*: Ibid., 6777–8.

135   During his childhood: This story is from Bank, pp. 293–300.

136   *We go behind*: Archive, 6726.

137   *The mother springbok*: Ibid., 7237–8.

137   *I sit here*: Ibid., 7239–41.

137   *From this direction*: Bleek & Lloyd, p. 287.

138   *He sits up*: Ibid., p. 387.

142   *For we seemed*: Archive, 4412.

145   *valuable service*: Kiernan, p. 236.

147   For chapters XXV to XXVII I have made particular use of Marlene Winberg, *Annotations of Loss and Abundance*, 2011. I also made quite a few notes from Lucy Lloyd's notebooks, when I was in the UCT Jagger Library.

149   *The elephant killed*: Lloyd notebooks, 9225.

150   *We do not throw*: Ibid., 9799.

150   *The man's father*: Ibid., 9564.

151   *the white man's thing*: all quotations from Archive, 9141–233.

156   *My mother's father*: Bleek & Lloyd, p. 429.

167   *These ladies are*: Bennun, p. 310.

167   She remained determined: The information about Lucy Lloyd's later years up to her death in 1914 draws on Bank, pp. 373–86.

170   *all who met*: Julia Blackburn, *The White Men*, Orbis Publishing, 1979, p. 9.

172   *A person who dies*: Archive, 3445.

175   *We do not feel nice*: Ibid., 1529.

175   *The little bird*: Ibid., 9220.

177   *The men call*: Ibid., 7978–9.

181   *Therefore father told me*: Ibid., 5202–4.

184   *When we see*: Ibid., 9156.

185   *The jackal head*: Ibid., 736–8.

185   *The aardwolf marries*: Ibid., 354.

186   *The Bushmen, when*: Ibid., 2157.

187   *The drum which*: Bleek & Lloyd, p. 351.

189   *The people who die*: Archive, 6011.

192 *Up to 1860*: George McCall Theal, *History of South Africa*, 5 vols, 1889–1900, Vol. 5, p. 259.

192 *The Ostrich walks out*: Bleek & Lloyd, p. 139.

195 *Dia!kwain heard*: Archive, 5882.

195 *The baboons sing*: Ibid., 5998–6006.

216 *Rattling along, rattling along*: Ibid., 7000, 7226, 7256.

222 *A man, I do not*: quoted in Bennun, p. 189.

222 *My mother told me*: Archive, 4079, 4090–2.

223 *our people who*: Ibid., 5059.

224 *because they felt*: Ibid., 4410.

225 *The anteater said*: Ibid., 2158.

229 *The men lay dead*: Bennun, p. 288.

231 *When I was at my place*: All subsequent quotes on //Kabbo's intended return home come from Bleek & Lloyd, pp. 299–317.

232 *After father had died*: Archive, 5139–40.

233 *The Moon said*: Bleek & Lloyd, p. 63.

235 *The hammerkop bird*: Archive, 5779.

242 *The sun crossed over*: Ibid., 2211–13.

242 *The place becomes dry*: Ibid., 7450–1.

243 *He quickly died*: Ibid., 1162.

243 *grave earth tree*: Ibid., 9190.

244 *//Kabbo's brother dying*: Bleek & Lloyd, pp. 299–315.

244 *That wind which*: Archive, 6100–1.

246 *//kurru a !kuita*: Bleek & Lloyd, p. 227.

246 *The women pound*: Ibid., pp. 343–7.

247 *//Kabbo married*: Ibid., pp. 299–315.

247 *The people's houses*: Archive, 6703.

250 *The man kills*: Bleek & Lloyd, pp. 137–43.

251 *They cannot ask*: Archive, 218, 135.

251 *I do not hear*: Bleek & Lloyd, p. 237.

254 *Our friend is right*: Bennun, p. 251.

260 *When these Stars*: Bleek & Lloyd, p. 81.

260 *We sleep soundly*: Archive, 1935–48.

261 *And we slept*: Ibid., 4684.

267 *there are two farmers*: Bank, p. 301.

273 *The man climbs the mountain*: Archive, 297–304.

275 *The ostrich comes*: Ibid., 2543, 2551–2.

279 *I must go together*: Bleek & Lloyd, pp. 299–317.

Illustration Credits

Iziko: Iziko Museums of South Africa, Social History Collections

Llarec: Lucy Lloyd Archive, Resource and Exhibition Centre, University of Cape Town

UCTLB: Bleek and Lloyd Collection, Manuscripts and Archives Library, University of Cape Town

NLLB: National Library of South Africa, Cape Town

Acknowledgements

The Society of Authors very kindly gave me a travel grant which enabled me to get to the Cape and to make the journey into the Karoo.

In 2018, I was given Neil Bennun's mobile phone number and was suddenly talking to him somewhere in Norway. He put me in touch with a circle of people all involved with the Bleek–Lloyd Archive in one way or another and with that I was on the road.

Tanya Barben had been head of the Special Collections Department at the University of Cape Town where the bulk of the Archive is held. She welcomed me as a guest in her home and while I was staying with her, she arranged for me to meet her good friends Andrew Bank, John Parkington and Marlene Winberg, each of whom shared their particular knowledge and insight into the /Xam and the Bushman world.

The trip to the Karoo to visit /Xam sites was organised by the archaeologist Janette Deacon, who proved to be a wonderful guide. I also much appreciated the presence of our two other companions Roger Van Wyk and Paul Weinberg. Janette arranged for us to stay at the Ardbeidsvreug Farm which encompasses //Kabbo's ancestral home. Elrina Crafford was warm and welcoming and she shared her intimate knowledge of the land and close understanding of the /Xam way of life, which she had learnt from her own observations and from Nak, her late father.

Mark McGranaghan, who had been responsible for putting

together a complete transcript of the Bleek – Lloyd notebooks as part of his PhD thesis, very kindly gave me access to the PDF of his work.

José Manuel de Prada-Samper, who has done fascinating work collecting Bushmen stories and memories, shared his enthusiasm, his knowledge and his encouragement.

I stayed for a couple of days with my friend Tim Dee and his wife Claire Spottiswoode at their home south of Cape Town, and when I was not sure if I could get back to the UK because of Covid, they assured me that I could stay for as long as was needed. While I was with them I was able to meet their sometime neighbour, the linguistic anthropologist Kerry Jones.

I did not manage to meet Pippa Skotnes, even though she initially was going to be part of the trip to the Karoo, but I am deeply indebted to her magisterial book, *Claim to the Country: The Archive of Wilhelm Bleek and Lucy Lloyd*. Since my return to the UK Pippa has been most helpful in accessing some of the images I wished to include here. I also much appreciate the patient help I have received from Clive Kirkwood, Archivist of the Special Collections and Archives at the University of Cape Town Libraries, and Lailah Hisham, Collections Manager: Social History Collections at the Cape Town Iziko Museum.

Dan Franklin, my old editor at Cape for the last thirty years, was living close by during much of lockdown and he has been a quiet and encouraging presence and a first reader of this book.

In April 2021 I wrote to Dan Frank, my editor at Pantheon in New York, saying I was ready to send him the manuscript. He answered with his usual warmth, courtesy and enthusiasm, but warned me that he was very unwell. He died in May 2021.

It has been a pleasure working with my new editor at Cape, Bea Hemming, who has also been a lockdown neighbour. I very much appreciate the fact that Peter Ward has again contributed his keen designer's eye to the look of one of my books.

My agent Victoria Hobbs has followed my progress and waves of uncertainty, with her customary humour and encouragement.

My friend Hugh Brody has been both supportive and encouraging, reading and discussing the manuscript as it took shape.

My friend Jayne Ivimey has also followed the development of this book very closely and I have much appreciated her input and her enthusiasm.

It has been a strange intense task writing during the pandemic and *Dreaming the Karoo* is nothing like the book I had first imagined. I am hugely appreciative of all the help and encouragement I have been given along the way, but any mistakes or omissions are entirely my own.